THE PERMISSIBLE LIE

The Inside Truth About Advertising

Samm Sinclair Baker

BEACON PRESS BOSTON

Beacon Series in Contemporary Communications
David Manning White, *General Editor*

Explorations in Communication, edited by Edmund Carpenter and Marshall McLuhan
The Mechanical Bride, by Marshall McLuhan
Sight, Sound, and Society, edited by David Manning White and Richard Averson
Mass Communications and American Empire, by Herbert I. Schiller
The Opinionmakers, by William L. Rivers
The Adversaries: Politics and the Press, by William L. Rivers
Culture for the Millions? edited by Norman Jacobs
Open to Criticism, by Robert Lewis Shayon
The Permissible Lie, by Samm Sinclair Baker

First published as a Beacon Paperback in 1971 by arrangement with the author

Beacon Press books are published under the auspices of the Unitarian Universalist Association
Published simultaneously in Canada by Saunders of Toronto, Ltd.
International Standard Book Number: 0–8070–6173–5

Contents

Contents

Chapter

WHAT'S THE "INSIDE" TRUTH ABOUT ADVERTISING?

1

"A new Renaissance must come, and a much greater one than that in which we stepped out of the Middle Ages; a great Renaissance in which mankind discovers that the ethical is the highest truth and the highest practicality, and experiences at the same time its liberation from that miserable obsession by what it calls reality, in which it has hitherto dragged itself along."

—ALBERT SCHWEITZER

The public has been fed two opposite views about advertising. Books such as *The Hidden Persuaders* by Vance Packard and other exposers look in from the *outside* at the notably weird world of advertising. The authors contend that people are the dupes of Madison Avenue supermen. These books picture the public as a puppet who performs when his advertising masters manipulate the strings.

The opposite view of advertising is presented by agency presidents David Ogilvy, Rosser Reeves, and other leading admen who have their own axes to grind. Their writings are primarily interested in presenting the achievements of their own agencies, to prove that "my agency is better than the other fellow's." These books avoid realistic criticism of undesirable advertising and business aspects. They have been pointedly summed up by one adman: "Nobody *active in advertising* is going to reveal anything that will lose accounts for his agency."

Another factor is the constant outpouring of praise for advertising. Every year there are speeches, articles, and "public-service advertisements" telling how pure advertising is, how advertisers operate primarily in the public interest. Only rarely do you hear an outspoken adman concede that some ads may be "slight exaggerations." This is akin to saying that a girl is "slightly" pregnant.

Each of these differing views contains some truth. But half-truths are often falsifications of the total facts. *What is the whole truth, the inside truth?*

Addressing the Association of National Advertisers' 57th Annual Meeting, a leading advertising executive, John W. Hobson, stated:

> Because our advertising reflects on a gigantic screen, every day, everywhere, the problems of our society, it is treated, by people who have not thought the matter through, as if it were the cause of those problems. . . . Sometimes I feel it is like one of those magnifying mirrors for shaving which enlarges to hideous proportions the wrinkles and blemishes of the face. But it is only reporting the facts.

By reporting only those "facts" that praise the product and ignoring reality that includes negative facts, advertising reflects a pervasive image of *untruth* in the "magnifying mirrors" of Madison Avenue, enlarged "to hideous proportions."

You, the public, cannot escape the bombardment of advertisements in your morning and evening newspapers, in most every magazine, the radios in your cars and homes, television's omnipresent glassy eye. You open your morning mail: Advertisements cascade out. You pick up a pack of matches: You're holding an ad. As you drive out in the country your eyes are assaulted by gaudy billboards. . . .

You bask on a sunny beach enjoying yourself, until you look up and see a skywriting plane belching out: YOU LOOK BURNED—COOL IT WITH NOXZEMA. Perhaps the pen you use to write a love letter proclaims itself as a gift of the People's Bank for Savings. The last strains of soothing music from your bedside radio are interrupted by ratcheting jingles: "Mr. Clean . . . Mr. Clean . . . Mr. Clean. . . ."

Who is to blame for this tasteless and irritating advertising barrage? Is there any solution?

For over thirty years I have been seeking constructive answers, and consciously and unconsciously writing this book. An item in my journal on September 8, 1933 summarized my ambitions and hopes: "Advertising seems more interesting to me than most any other way of making a living. I hope to earn enough money from it so that eventually I can enlighten the public about its grave evils as well as its benefits. My purpose will be to help eliminate those evils and enlarge its benefits for the whole nation." Ever since, I have been making notes and gathering material, enough to fill over ten books.

Four years ago I left Madison Avenue to devote myself to full-time writing. My conclusions after more than thirty years' experience boil down to this:

First, the overwhelming aim of advertising is to make a profit; to serve the public best becomes a secondary consideration and *is confined within the limits of the profit motivation.* A lie that helps build profits is considered a permissible lie. Of course, the lie must not be so blatant that it results in eventual damage to the company's profits.

Second, a substantial amount of advertising is based on the concept of the permissible lie.

Third, this fakery, through saturation and repetition, undermines the attitudes and ethics of the adult, the child, and the family.

Fourth, and highly important, I am convinced that the immoral concept of the permissible lie is not necessary to achieve the improved sales and profits the advertiser demands.

Admen may complain that the revelations which follow make them scapegoats, responsible for all public ills, once again. On the other hand, they boast that no field is so influential on the public mind and actions as the "communications business." That is true; and they should place the responsibilities of advertising square in the middle of the public spotlight—for examination.

Advertising is permeated with "permissible lies," such as this example of one of the many types that will be delineated on these pages: A neighbor set out to clean a soiled mirror. He explained, "I used a nationally advertised glass cleaner because I'd often seen on TV how you spray and wipe clean in seconds. So I sprayed and wiped . . . and wiped . . . and wiped, finishing 10 minutes later."

He asked his wife, "Why doesn't it work like they show on TV?" She said, "It's a fake like many other kinds of products. I keep switching brands, hoping one will live up to the advertising."

I asked a friend at the agency that did the glass cleaner advertising, "Did the people who created the commercials ever use the product at home?" He shrugged, "Probably not. But if we showed that you have to apply elbow grease, nobody would buy the brand because competitors are faking it too. That's advertising—you know as well as I do."

To understand advertising requires a clear examination of how advertising people on the inside operate. Without that insight, one cannot estimate the effects of advertising on our daily lives.

A fundamental truth about advertising is that advertising agency people are *not* the ultimate decision-makers. As the advertising agency system functions today, *they* are the puppets, the manipulated. Nor is the advertiser as he sits astride the bleeding, panting agencyman the one who wields the whip in full command.

The final control, the decisive power, is in *your* hands and under *your* command—*if you will use it.*

How the advertising business *really operates* will prove this conclusively.

Chapter 2

HOW THE MADISON AVENUE RAT RACE FUNCTIONS

Why is Madison Avenue a rat race?

While in the business I naturally soft-pedaled my answer to that question. But every adman knows that advertising is indeed a scurrying rat race in which the incredible is commonplace and the unbelievable is true. The basis for this is the advertiser/agency system. The advertising agency is in fact as well as in name the *agent* of the advertiser. The agency serves the advertiser's desires and needs, and receives 15-percent commission on the total dollars spent in television, radio, magazines, newspapers, billboards, and practically all other media.

The advertiser says, "Here are x dollars. Let's see your plan on how to spend them." Sometimes the agency is also asked to suggest how much the budget should be to produce the desired sales and profits. Out of every $1 million the advertiser spends on television, for example, the agency receives $150,000. From this commission, the agency maintains offices, pays salaries, and makes its profit.

There is a slowly increasing trend toward compensating the agency through a fee rather than by the 15-percent commission on the total expenditure. The aim of a fee system is to pay the agency for the amount of work involved instead of a fixed percentage which may result in excessive or inadequate rewards. Whatever the method of computing payment, the significant point is that the advertiser is the boss.

The final decision on the quality and substance of the advertising is his alone.

If you're offended or angered by a campaign and want to know whom to blame, look to the advertiser. The agencyman is only his front runner. The agency creates the campaign, whether it is based on truth, fakery, or drivel. The advertiser accepts, amends, or rejects it. Often, the ads are patterned after a directive by the advertiser. There's painful realism in a cartoon showing Mr. Big pulling a note out of the suggestion box and saying, "Here's a great idea. It's from me."

Except in rare cases in which there is an ironbound contract or a special obligation, the advertiser can fire the agency almost as easily as he can snap his fingers. That is why Madison Avenue is known as Ulcer Gulch. Agencies scramble all over one another in a ceaseless, frenzied rat race to get more clients, to add millions to their billing, and to increase their 15-percent take of the total.

Lee Bristol of Bristol-Myers is credited with the statement that the frenetic adman can be described in five words: "Yes, sir! No, sir! Ulcer!"

When my first mystery novel, a burlesque of advertising, was published, Joseph Kaselow in his New York *Herald Tribune* advertising news column noted: "The title, *One Touch of Blood,* won't impress admen—they see it running in rivers every day."

A public-relations man at General Electric Company, Harry R. Gasker, wrote in *Printers' Ink,* an advertising trade magazine: "To many advertising account executives, chronic nervous dyspepsia, psychosomatic tension, and hyperacidity are more than just medical words used in television commercials. These are very real terms that describe what is probably the most common occupational disease of the advertising game." He named as the most important cause: *client frightitis.* An agency executive echoed unhappily, "We're in a passionate business."

This Madison Avenue affliction is evident daily in conference rooms of agencies across the country. Some conferences involving a few key men are effective and valuable;

most comprise a common blend of confusion, crisis, fakery, and ineptitude.

Species of participants at an agency conference usually include, according to adman Jack James, "the Scarlet-Throated Mumbler, the Gray Flannel Easel, the Double-Breasted Note-Passer, the Tufted Table Pounder, and the Slate-Blue Pipe Smoker." They are also known as executive, creative, account service, media, television department people, production men and women, and miscellaneous other types.

A typical agency conference is set for 11 A.M. Its purpose is to help create and build a campaign that the client will okay. This "small meeting" involves twelve people. No one who has ever been to one of these conferences arrives by 11 A.M. The minions of lowest status and salary start drifting in a few minutes after the hour. With luck all are assembled by 11:20, but there's always at least one who stamps in at 11:21 and mutters to the head man (he's the agency president at this meeting), "Goddamned client had me on the phone for a half hour; couldn't get rid of him."

This causes the president to turn yellow-green, reach for his pillbox, and gasp, "Everything all right?"

The late arrival settles in his chair, lights a cigarette, throws the match so that it just misses the ashtray—intentionally. He shrugs, "I pacified him, put out the brushfire. It looks good but"—he glances around at the others—"let's discuss it when we break up here."

As an afterthought he adds, "Sorry I'm late." He has established his superiority over the others by keeping them waiting, by still being warm from contact with The Client, by having arranged for a personal discussion with the president. (Investigation would probably show that he has been waiting out the past twenty minutes in the men's room.)

Many in the meeting are now angry because of the latecomer's downmanship and the wasted time chopped from their pressured routines. Most are seething because the conference is now sure to run long, making them late for their luncheon dates.

In this antagonistic atmosphere, the account supervisor outlines the proposed campaign. He's the main contact man with the client. He used to be known a few years ago as the account executive; his assistant was the assistant account executive. But someone got the bright idea that if the account executive was called the account supervisor, then the assistant account executive could become the account executive, and the ex-college boy who carried the portfolios could be designated as assistant account executive. Thus the agency with three "Executives" heading the account seems to be giving much more service to the client.

When the account supervisor finishes his presentation, each of the conferees considers his response in this order:

First, what comment, if any, will be best for my prestige and standing, as regarded by the president?

Second, what can I say that won't leave my neck sticking out?

Third, what contribution will be best for the agency and advertiser?

As soon as one person gives his opinion, almost all must get into the act—otherwise they might be considered dummies with nothing to contribute. Therefore, each speaks up, even if only to say, "The proposition is so much blue sky [a safe descriptive] that I can't make any productive statement at this time [I'll pitch in later, when there's less risk]."

If the president's reaction seems negative, one is likely to venture, "I see flaws here," or the safer, "I pass. I need more time to think about it." If the president shows that he's in favor, it's common to switch to, "On the other hand, the campaign could be saved if"—and then he proposes what he thinks the president is for.

Each department head is asked to give his findings. For instance, the director of research was scheduled toward the beginning, but five others managed to wedge in their presentations first. He waves a thick binder. "I need at least an hour to present all this material—"

The president snaps, "Give us the gist of it in ten minutes, tops."

The research director reads monotonously for fifteen minutes, then is cut short by questions, objections, and a general bombardment of overlapping comments. For again, everyone wants to be heard, sensibly or otherwise.

The president's voice slices through the uproar, "Whoa, damnit! Let's get on with it! I got ten minutes by the clock, then I gotta run."

The creative director presents some proposed ads. They may be greeted with enthusiasm (rarely), by mild comment ("damned with faint praise"), or by vigorous objections that result in a flat turndown. Usually, some men are for and some opposed, unless the president takes a stand, in which case, everyone is likely to vote his way. If the theme of the ads is the client's idea, general approval comes in a hurry. If it is contrary to the client's expressed views, it hasn't a chance, for if it doesn't get his approval, it won't appear on TV, in magazines, on radio; it's nowhere.

Trying to please the client, with a crumb of his suggestions incorporated here and a compromise there, usually results in a patched-up campaign which has neither spark, sense, nor conviction. This hodgepodge is generally completely different from the original concept, good or bad, based on extensive creative thinking and research.

Adding to the confusion at agencies is a plans board of top executives who kill or pass campaigns about which they know very little. Herb Lubalin, an independent spirit once elected Art Director of the Year, explained: "The plans board is the buffer state between client and agency. Its job is to keep him always in great expectation of the great things to come, which it then keeps from ever materializing."

After a few bewildering months of working in an agency, attending many conferences, a young ex-football star halfback was asked how he liked the business. "Well," he said, "you go into a conference like into a football huddle—figuring you'll learn just where to carry the ball. But," he shook his head dazedly, "by the time the meeting is over you find that they've moved the goal posts."

A first conference is frequently followed by similar confused meetings. More compromises are effected. The ads are weakened further or far-out insanities are added. Finally the campaign is ready for presentation to the client in a conference of agency and advertiser executives.

For this agency/advertiser meeting at 11 A.M., the agency "team" is seated by 10:50 sharp. The confrontation between advertiser and agency has been likened to the relationship between a knife and a throat. Cain and Abel have also been mentioned.

The last briefing by the agency head before the meeting generally goes something like this: "We must all reflect unwavering confidence to show we're not guessing but *know* this campaign is terrific and can't fail to sell the product most successfully. Of course, we can't be sure, nobody can. So what? Naturally I'll leave us a way out if the client objects. But until then nobody says a single goddamn word of doubt about our presentation—right?"

The client group arrives at 11:10 or later to emphasize who is boss. Now comes a period of charm talk about the most recent golf game, the week's football or baseball scores, and a blast at whatever political party the client hates. Abruptly the client head shifts gears: "Let's get to the business of this meeting. What've you got to show us?"

Instantly, the agencymen hop to their presentation. First, page after page of data "lay the groundwork," until finally come the sample ads, beautifully and expensively mounted, representative of the complete campaign.

The proposed ads are seldom approved in their original form. If the client is less than happy about the ideas, the usual reaction from the agency head is a hasty, "You certainly have a point there, T. J. The agency will take another hard look at the material. Let's pack up shop now and get an early start on lunch. I, for one, am pretty damned thirsty, ha-ha. Over lunch at the Pavillon we can set a date for showing you a revise, incorporating your excellent suggestions. This has been a most valuable session, a fine interchange of ideas. Many, many thanks."

This means that a completely new campaign must be created, usually within a week (and weekend) of frenzied activity. It will be based on the client's comments and hopefully will get an okay. It all adds up to this:

The one essential, driving aim of the agency's campaign is not to please and sell you, the public, but to sell the advertiser and get his initialed okay. The public is a poor also-ran.

Chapter

IS ADVERTISING TRUTH, HALF-TRUTH—OR LESS?

3

Ask admen and you'll find them agreeing eagerly with Chaucer that "truth is the highest thing that man may keep." Why then doesn't advertising hew to the truth?

One reason is that advertising is aimed toward a single dominating goal: To sell the goods. *Advertising Age* stated: ". . . those holding ad competitions awards should make sales objectives and sales results the No. 1 criterion. After all, that's what the whole business of advertising is about . . ." first, last, and only.

To increase sales, most anything goes—misrepresentation, deception, lies—unless actionable. The approach is usually to produce the hardest-selling campaign without perpetrating recognizable fraud. This attitude inevitably breeds the permissible lie—the half-truth, of which it has been said: "A half-truth is generally the worst half."

An adman will sugar-coat this charge with the contention that "Advertising is the art of wrapping the truth in imagination." Unfortunately, too much advertising consists of wrapping the truth with little imagination. Confronted with charges that much advertising is deceptive, admen usually counter indignantly, "Our ads don't lie."

"Do your ads tell the whole truth? Do they even tell 51 percent of the truth?"

"How the hell can anybody expect a company to tell the whole truth in its advertising? Or even 51 percent of the truth? Our ads have to sell the goods or we're sunk!"

Why does the tag on nationally advertised Mary Jane Dresses read: "NO IRONING! NO FOOLING!"? For just one reason—because so many advertisers who originally promised "no ironing" were indeed fooling. When "permanent press" came along, women were wary because they had been fooled so often in the past. Advertisers like Bloomingdale's department store had to reach for a bigger-than-before lure: "NOW TRULY NO-IRON. . . ."

During my years in advertising I fooled myself. I was aware of fakery, of course. But I didn't realize consciously the vast amount of "fraud" perpetrated in ads, including many of my own efforts. The adman becomes so accustomed to using the permissible lie that it becomes his natural approach in creating an ad and selling a product.

Here is typical copy for a deodorant soap: "You haven't got a worry in the world when you start the day with [this soap]. Because it wipes out skin bacteria that cause odor. All day long." Scientists advise that this is not possible—and, of course, so do makers of deodorant sticks, sprays, creams, and whatnots. Some users, after a hectic day, said, "Not true about deodorant soaps." Others said that they didn't know, because one is not usually aware of odor on oneself—which is why the advertisers got away with such claims. Give an advertiser an inch and he'll drive through a yard of "iffy" promises.

Within the confines of the industry, Louis Brockway, vice president of Young and Rubicam (Number 3 agency in size), upbraided an audience of advertising people: "We must eliminate from advertising the half-truths, the insincere comparatives, the fraudulent claims and misleading assertions."

Confronted with a reading of this statement recently, a group of admen reluctantly nodded in agreement. One voiced the consensus opinion: "All of us want to clean up deception in advertising. We're making big advances. We'll soon get rid of all the fraud. That kind of frank talk will accomplish it." They were then informed that Brockway had made the speech over twelve years ago.

Inside the agency the basic approach is hardly conducive to truth-telling. The usual thinking in forming a campaign is first, what can we say, true or not, that will sell the product best? The second consideration is, how can we say it effectively and get away with it so that 1. people who buy won't feel let down by too big a promise that doesn't come true, and 2. the ads will avoid quick and certain censure by the Federal Trade Commission? (The FTC is the main government regulatory agency over advertising.)

The predominating consideration then is "How much can we get away with?" This is obvious in the false TV demonstrations where producers feel they can "get by with it." A landmark case involved Colgate-Palmolive Company's Rapid Shave Cream. The commercial showed "sandpaper" being shaved while a voice explained: "To prove Rapid Shave's super-moisturizing power, we put it right from the can onto this rough, dry sandpaper. It was apply, soak—and off in a stroke."

This was very impressive if you felt you had a "sandpaper beard." But the rough, dry sandpaper was not sandpaper; it was a sheet of Plexiglas to which sand had been applied. Tests showed that actual sandpaper had to be soaked in Rapid Shave for about eighty minutes—not for the few seconds depicted in the commercial—in order to be shaved.

It finally took a Supreme Court decision written by Chief Justice Warren to check such "deceptive trade practices" which had first been challenged by the Federal Trade Commission. Colgate-Palmolive and its agency, Ted Bates and Company (Number 5), had fought the FTC objections as unfair and inhibiting. A spokesman for the advertiser commented after the final decision, "Now we and all other advertisers will know what the rules are in this field." Could anyone believe that the rules had granted permission to deceive?

Inside the agencies, many admen complained that the decision prevented even truthful demonstrations. On this point, the Supreme Court majority decision stated: "We think it inconceivable that the ingenious advertising world will be unable, if it so desires, to conform to the commission's insistence that the public be not misinformed."

In another classic instance, investigation proved that a TV commercial by Libbey-Owens-Ford to demonstrate that no distortion in the glass occurred *with the car window rolled down.* The company stated that it directed its advertising agency, Fuller and Smith and Ross (Number 27), to produce an effective commercial, and didn't know that an open window was being used. In another commercial, the FTC also noted that Vaseline had been rubbed on a house window to exaggerate the distortion of the glass in comparison with Libbey-Owens-Ford safety plate glass—and that in any case the plate glass used in cars is not the same as the plate glass used in a house window. The Federal Court of Appeals upheld the FTC complaint.

On the popular WNBC-TV "Tonight" program, star Johnny Carson asked why the ice cream in a commercial for Smucker's Butterscotch Topping didn't melt. Announcer Ed McMahon explained that the ice cream was actually a vegetable spread for cooking. Said Carson, "There ought to be a certain amount of honesty, you know. They do that in many commercials. When they show that woman cleaning that floor and say, 'One swipe to it,' did you ever see that floor? It's the filthiest thing you have ever seen and they go right through. One swipe and it's clean. They put graphite on that floor, powdered graphite."

Mary Carter Paints advertised for some fifteen years "BUY A CAN AND GET THE SECOND CAN FREE." The FTC charged that Mary Carter ads were deceptive because the only price offered, in the absence of any other prices, was really the price for two cans. The company fought the action all the way. The Supreme Court ruled: "It was marketing twins, and in allocating what is in fact the price of two cans to one can, yet calling one 'free,' Mary Carter misrepresented."

A successful businessman said, "If you're going to succeed in advertising, you must give the public the illusion that they're getting the better of you." This is certainly true in respect to cents-off and other so-called bargain offers. They give shoppers the feeling that they've cut the advertiser's profits to the bone. Actually the advertiser has already figured a nice profit, even at the cents-off price. That's why cents-off is called "fictitious pricing" by the FTC where investigation shows that the cents-off price is the *usual* price. The biggest advertisers are among the offenders.

This is also commonplace procedure with some higher-priced items: The advertiser prices the product to retail at $25, and sells it for a while at that price, less 40 percent to the retailer. He then cuts the retail price to about $15, less 40 percent to the retailer. He still makes a profit because that's how he figured his price set-up in the first place. Retailers offer the item: "Was $25, now yours for $15." The purchaser feels he's getting a great bargain. Actually $15 is the "normal" price for the item with a fair profit for the advertiser, wholesaler, and retailer.

Before believing an advertiser's guarantee (often specific and valid), you had best check it. About a common type of infraction, the FTC stated: "Contrary to Accro's claims that its watches are 'Bonded' and are accompanied by a 'Guarantee Bond,' it has not executed a bond, insurance policy or agreement . . . for the purpose of assuring fulfillment of the terms of its guarantee" and that furthermore the "guarantee is deceptive because it does not disclose the nature and extent of the guarantee."

A new ruling had to be put into effect that advertisers of TV sets could only give the "actual size of the viewable picture area." This was necessary because deceptive ads were promising the overall dimensions of the picture tube as picture size, even though some of the area is blocked off at the edges when the tube is installed. Other ads gave the *diagonal* dimension of the picture without explaining that it was about an inch more than the width even before the edges were trimmed by the frame.

Optical illusions are another form of the permissible lie. A competitor claimed that a Simmons mattress ad showed photos comparing a "narrow" competitive mattress with a "just right" Simmons. He said that Simmons used an extra-wide headboard with the competing mattress, and that actually there was very little difference between the two mattresses. It pays to check exact details in inches, net weights, etc., lest you be fooled by implications in the advertising that do not exist in fact.

Is it true, as some claim, that the deceitful practices of a *very few* advertisers give the entire field a bad name? Stockton Helffrich, manager of the New York code office of the National Association of Broadcasters, answered in a speech to the inner fraternity. He denied the "hackneyed myth [that] the false and deceptive advertising practices of a few smear the good practices of the majority."

He emphasized, "I wonder whether one could not as readily presume an opposite argument: the gray-area practices of the majority of advertisers blur the sunny virtues of a minority elite. The fact is that too substantial a number of advertisers who stretch the boundaries of truthfulness simply never get caught."

Consider this radio commentator's report: "Castro made a speech today in which he said that Cuba's sugar production would go up ten million tons a year. However he didn't say *when*. Since Cuba can't reach this production for years, the statement was obviously misleading, a sugar pill to pacify his people. . . ."

Many advertisers would say that the claim is not deception, just an acceptable half-truth. Castro didn't say that production would go up ten million tons a year *this* year. Yes, but he implied it. Advertising frequently is guilty of this same kind of misrepresentation, the lie of omission.

Merck & Co., Inc. advertised that "Remarkable Sucrets lozenges relieve sore-throat pain fast and kill even staph and strep germs." FTC hearing examiner Edgar A. Buttle said that such ads are likely to deceive people because they imply thorough killing power and fail to disclose that germs in the throat tissues, which contribute to the infection, are not touched. He added, "Every manufacturer has a subjective sense about his own product which makes objective analysis difficult where imaginative advertising is prescribed by an advertising agent."

This truism, which was confirmed for me over the years, led a wag to call advertising "breach of promise"; it might also be labeled "breach of premise." Not only the advertiser but also the agency people deceive themselves, along with the public, as they come to believe even absurd claims about their cherished profit-making product.

Revco stores in Detroit and Cleveland advertised that their products were approved for quality and value by the "Consumer Protective Institute" and thus earned the "CPI Seal." The FTC investigated and revealed that the Consumer Protective Institute was created by the advertising agency, and that CPI had never tested anything.

Viewers have complained of getting tired blood from Geritol commercials about "tired blood." One commercial showed a completely worn-out husband. Then he took Geritol and was out dancing with his wife, as the announcer promised: "In only one day Geritol iron is in your bloodstream, carrying strength and energy to every part of your body." The FTC stated that only a small fraction of Geritol iron is in the bloodstream in twenty-four hours, that no more than 10 percent of the population suffers from iron deficiency, and that "there is little relationship between the tiredness symptoms and iron deficiency." Five years after the FTC tried to stop such claims, Geritol was still battling in the courts, and tired-blood advertising was still flowing over the TV tubes.

Bewildering claims and counterclaims abound in the field of analgesics—pain-relievers such as aspirin—on which Americans spend nearly a half billion dollars annually, spurred by almost $100 million in advertising. A Bayer magazine ad stated: "For speed and strength of relief, Bayer Aspirin is unsurpassed by any product tested, including the so-called 'extra-strength' one that claims to be 50 percent stronger." In the same magazine, "the extra-strength pain-reliever," Excedrin, claims, "tablet for tablet, 50 percent stronger than aspirin." Concurrently on TV: "Bufferin delivers twice as much pain reliever twice as fast as aspirin." Anacin advertised: "Strongest in the pain reliever doctors recommend most." Clearly somebody is lying. The FTC contended that "each of the various analgesic products . . . is effective to essentially the same degree as all other products supplying an equivalent quantity of an analgesic ingredient or combination of ingredients."

Alka-Seltzer advertising promised the best antacid product "you can buy without a prescription." I wrote to both Alka-Seltzer and Bromo-Seltzer for clarification about this claim. A letter from Alka-Seltzer's associate medical director, Dr. William C. Luther, repeated their claim to "best." On the other hand, Bromo-Seltzer's product manager, John W. Amerman, wrote that the situation "has been a source of great concern to all of us. . . . Our studies continue to show that Bromo-Seltzer is the most effective antacid product you can purchase without a prescription." Whom is the buyer to believe? I asked an agencyman connected with the Alka-Seltzer agency about the validity of their "best" claim. He shrugged and said, "It sure is helping to sell a lot of product."

A large chain food market was fined $250 for having featured and sold "lowly flounder fillets as epicurean English fillets of gray sole." The judge brushed aside the store's explanation that it was done by mistake. He said, "I have found in my experience in this court that no misrepresentation occurs as a matter of accident."

One of the nation's leading department stores was accused of advertising men's clothing that had been the overstock of a comparatively small Florida store, offered at sale prices in New York. Investigation showed that a small percentage of the sale clothes had been in the Florida store. The rest had been manufactured expressly for the New York sale, had never been offered in the Florida store. The department store heads blamed the buyer for the "conspiracy." They fired him after the store was accused of publishing "false and misleading advertising."

Admen insist that implication doesn't constitute misrepresentation. Is it deceptive to imply magical properties in the advertising of skin creams containing mystical elements—"royal jelly," for example? One ad offered: "Super-Royal Cream . . . Nature's most mysterious gift to beauty. Mysterious because Royal Jelly has always defied complete analysis—but a wonderful gift to beauty for the countless women who have experienced its beautifying effect on their skins."

The book, *1001 Questions and Answers to Your Skin Problems,* by Doctors Sidney and Stephanie Robbins, dermatologists, and myself, states that any benefit from royal jelly for the skin "has not been proved. The royal jelly is said to have originated with the queen bee. A wit commented that many women have been stung by the high costs of the creams with royal jelly." Another dermatologist said, "Royal jelly is of less known value than common petroleum jelly."

An adman reacted, "What's the difference? Women like to be fooled about the goo they smear on their faces. So we fool them. They love it!"

Armour advertised: "ONE POUND OF ARMOUR STAR FRANKS IS AS NOURISHING AS ONE POUND OF STEAK." The inference is clear that when you eat frankfurters you're getting as much nourishment as when you eat a pound of steak. But—did you ever try eating the ten average-size frankfurters in a pound package—as one meal?

Madison Avenue contends that such advertising sleight-of-hand is perfectly permissible. Admen fail to see the similarity between their presentation and an item from the bulletin published by inmates of Kentucky State Penitentiary: A prisoner who had been very successful in a termite exterminating business until caught said he had conducted his trade "honestly" except for one little twist: He always carried a little bottle of termites with him to spread around just in case he couldn't find any in the house.

Similarly, loosing "just a few termites" undermines the entire structure of belief in advertising. If you catch a person in a "little" lie, you're inclined not to believe anything he says thereafter. That accounts for the frequent comment, "All ads are a pack of lies."

A particularly flagrant case of advertising fraud is that of Regimen Tablets, a product claimed to be so effective as an appetite depressant that users could lose weight without dieting or giving up "favorite foods." A newspaper dubbed this "The $16 Million Reducing-Pill Hoax."

Those accused of violating Food and Drug Administration (FDA, not FTC) regulations fraudulently were brought to trial. During the proceedings, "puffery"—that favorite Madison Avenue alibi word—was defined by an agency executive witness as "the dramatic extension of a claim area." The defense attorney elaborated that puffery "is a normal, accepted, routine practice in the advertising industry."

One example he gave of legitimate or permissible puffery was the retouching of a woman's hips in an "after" photo for the narrower effect desired. By this criterion it is puffery rather than fraud when a woman's hips are slimmed by an artist's brush, rather than by dieting pills as promised (no retouching brush was included with the package of dieting pills).

Presiding Judge Bartels observed: "There is no principle of law that I know of condoning puffery as a justification for deception. *Caveat emptor* (let the buyer beware) is no longer acceptable." *Caveat emptor* is frequently the rule on Madison Avenue.

Regimen ads featured before-and-after photos and testimonials. The indictment charged that endorsers actually lost weight by starvation diets and medication. One of the models, Mrs. Dorothy Bryce, testified that she was told by agency representatives not to look happy and not to stand up straight for her "before Regimen" photo. In the TV commercials she stated that she reduced from a size sixteen to a size twelve and "ate what I liked, even desserts." In the witness chair she said this was not true, that she finally ate only black coffee, phenobarbitol, and a thyroid extract. When asked by the agency TV producer how she was feeling, she answered, "Fine. Get the ambulance." But on TV, Mrs. Bryce said that she "never felt better."

The assistant U.S. Attorney General called the campaign

"one of the most brazen frauds ever perpetrated on the public, mostly women." A man at the Regimen agency alibied, "Thousands of other advertisers and agencies are doing the same kind of thing. We just happen to be the fall guys that the government picked on."

In my experience, the agency—except in rare cases—is just as aware as the client if the claim is questionable. Agencymen are usually willing, even eager, to go along without question. Long before there was any government action, I discussed the Regimen campaign with other admen. All agreed that the ads couldn't be telling the truth. Nevertheless, TV, radio, magazines, and newspapers accepted and ran the obviously deceptive advertising.

The innocent word "new" becomes very tricky in advertising because admen are convinced that you'll try anything labeled "new" and/or "improved," whether it actually is or not. Maxwell House Instant Coffee was advertised as "A New Coffee Discovery" for many years. The same advertisement was repeated year after year with little or no change. The "new" stayed in even as the ads grew old. An adman defended this, "After all, the *New* Testament is almost two thousand years old." An ad acclaimed the Pontiac car as not only "new" but also "newnew" and "newnewnew." Dodge touted its Polara model as "allnew."

The FTC finally set six months as the tentative "outer limit" of newness. Admen screamed in protest. *Advertising Age* editorialized: "The newness of the New Year is lost in a matter of seconds; but New England is still called that after nearly 400 years, and New Mexico is still 'new' after more than 400. . . . And the New World, geologists say, is probably two billion years old. Yet it would create confusion to start calling it the Old World, since there already is one." Obviously all the protests add up to a defense of deception in advertising.

A housewife inundated with all the claims by products that they are "Now New! Improved!" observed, "It makes me wonder just how horrible the stuff was that they used to try to sell me."

In a typical meeting, an advertiser told agencymen: "Our top canned item is slipping. We need some new excitement in the advertising. We're going to redesign the label to give it a new look. So come up with a 'New! Improved!' campaign—lots of big-big promise. Show us layouts in a week so we can move fast."

Someone asked, "Anything new or improved *inside* the can?"

The client glared. "What the hell kind of a question is that? I'd have said so if we'd made any changes other than the label. That'll be redesigned and the product will *look* new and improved, won't it? Whose side are you on anyhow?"

The questioner wasn't on any side very long. He was fired from the agency.

Chapter

CLUES TO COMMON TYPES OF TRICKERY

4

"Only truth smells sweet forever," wrote a philosopher, "and illusions are deadly as a cankerworm." Admen frequently use tricks of illusion and distortion, knowing that the eye is quicker than the ear, as in TV commercials like the following:

In a Bayer Aspirin commercial exposed repeatedly to millions, the announcer said: "Yes, aspirin is what doctors recommend. . . ." He simultaneously held up a package of Bayer Aspirin. He didn't *say* that doctors recommend Bayer, but this is the impression the viewers I questioned received from his gesture. Such "innocent" misleading stratagems are a specific part of many TV commercials.

The ad-lib radio commercial contributes to this problem. Here is a sequence by the popular team of Klavan and Finch on a leading New York station, WNEW:

"I wouldn't be here if it weren't for Bayer Aspirin."

"Oh, you felt terrible and Bayer made you well enough?"

"No. It takes a certain number of commercials to pay our salaries, and Bayer is one of the best-paying sponsors. So if it wasn't for them I wouldn't be here."

"Hmmm. Well, anyhow, you were smart to take it because doctors say take Bayer Aspirin for a cold because it's the best," etc., etc.

Undoubtedly the copy prepared by Bayer's agency was: "Doctors say take aspirin for a cold." However the ad-lib boys said that doctors recommend Bayer specifically.

Admen generally know that ad-lib deejays (disc jockeys, record spinners) can get away with statements that would bring disapproval from government agencies. The ad-lib boys encourage this practice in order to get more advertising. There's very little chance of FTC inspectors listening and catching such infractions. If caught, the adman shows the original "safe" copy and says, "Sorry, the ad-lib boys went overboard in their enthusiasm. We'll caution them to make sure it never happens again."

Meanwhile, back at the station, an agencyman is telling the deejays, "Look, fellows, if you want to slant the commercial a little, exaggerate some, the sponsor won't mind at all." While some agencymen frown on this trickery, it's practically standard procedure as agencies strive to please the sponsor.

I met a disc jockey at a party a few days after I'd heard him tell on the radio how much his family loves "Popsies." I said, "We tried them at home and sent the remainder off to the advertiser and got our money back. We thought they tasted like shredded cardboard seasoned with glue."

"So did we," he said, "but 'sincere' personal endorsement is my stock in trade."

A tricky approach often used is the line, "There's nothing just like—" as in "THERE'S NOTHING JUST LIKE SEGO," Pet Milk's reducing product. A dozen other items are very much like Sego, which followed Metrecal's success. True, none is "just like" Sego. The intent is to make you think it's much different and has a special magic which cannot be duplicated by others.

Other examples of this gambit: "THIS IS COLOR TELEVISION AS ONLY SYLVANIA MAKES IT." It may not be the best, as the statement implies, but it's truly "as only Sylvania makes it." Another: "NO OTHER SHORTENING HAS CRISCO'S FORMULA." A different brand of shortening may have a better formula, but it's not Crisco's. And: "NO OTHER VERMOUTH CAN ENDOW YOUR COCKTAILS WITH THE UNIQUE TASTE AND FLAVOR OF TRIBUNO." The "unique taste and flavor" may not be palatable, but it's definitely Tribuno's.

Note the word "stay" in all kinds of hackneyed copy—"stay slim," "stay healthy," "stay young." The inference is that the product will *make* you slim, healthy, or young. Analyzed, the promise is only that if you're now slim, healthy, and young, the item will help you *stay* that way.

Have you noticed the tricky comparative "er"? The advertiser has been warned that he can't promise that his product will "make you healthy." But he is permitted to say it will "keep you health*ier*." Healthier than what? Healthier than a product that contains cyanide?

"SCOTT [ScotTissue] MAKES IT BETTER FOR YOU." The "better" can mean most anything—better ingredients, better manufacture, better everything. Scott or any other manufacturer can't know this because they don't know all the competitors' ingredients, methods, and other vital information that establish superiority in fact as well as in words.

An advertiser may counter: " 'Better' means many things —that our products are better than they used to be, better than any other brand; if a toilet paper, better than sandpaper or carbon paper. We're not saying that our product is better than all others." But without question that's his purpose—otherwise the advertiser wouldn't spend millions on the claim.

Watch out for that treacherous word "helps." Government regulations have stopped advertisers from saying that a product "*cures* your cold." So copywriters switched to the glib "*helps* relieve your cold," "*helps* you stay slim." The announcer says loudly, "BRAND X WORKS FIFTEEN WAYS TO (*low*) help (*loud*) RELIEVE YOUR COLD!"

Constant subterfuge is employed by advertisers in comparisons with "other leading products." Lavoris mouthwash, a division of Vick Chemical Company, headlined: "TESTS CONFIRM ONE MOUTHWASH BEST AGAINST MOUTH ODOR." They know, just as surely as any adman does, that many people won't read any copy beyond the headline and the name Lavoris. Few note that only "the four leading mouthwashes" were compared, although any one of dozens on the market might be more effective than "best" Lavoris.

I sent for "a new scientific research report" offered in the ad, and a scientist friend questioned three points instantly: First, only sixty persons were tested and form too small a sample. Second, the technique requiring "no food or drink taken during three-hour test period" after using the mouthwash isn't normal living. Third, the testing method—"direct mouth-to-nose technique" (one person blows his breath into another's nose through a concealing curtain)—is highly unscientific.

Naturally you're never told of test projects that cost millions of dollars and are thrown out because they prove advertisers' products to be inferior to others. A cartoon showed a conference with one adman saying: "Seventeen hospitals tested our product and found it completely ineffectual—but we can still advertise it as 'hospital-tested.' "

A scientist told me that he had been offered three times his present university salary to become head of the "scientific research division" to be newly established by one of the largest advertising agencies. His conscience forced him to reject the offer—"I found that they didn't want to invest in comparative projects of scientific value. Their only aim was to prove some tiny edge of superiority for the product they handled. They didn't care if it was 90 percent inferior in most aspects and only 10 percent better in one; the latter is all they would disclose. That would be 'truthful' but only as far as it went, and *untruthful* in total. I call this 'iceberg research,' where only a small part of the entire finding is revealed to the onlooker. I couldn't buy that—my family isn't that hungry."

What is deliberately left out of an ad can result in grave deception. In October, 1966, the FDA took action to force revisions in medical journal ads of Upjohn Company's Lincocin, a fast-selling new prescription drug. The FDA stated that while the ads emphasized that the product would not cause kidney or nervous disorders, they did not stress equally that use sometimes resulted in severe diarrhea and blood poisoning; and that the ads did not advise doctors that sensitivity tests are recommended. Other drug firms were accused of similar serious omissions in their ads. An observer labeled such advertising as *"renditions of the truth."*

Listerine, Micrin, and other mouthwashes make patently exaggerated promises that use of their product spells the difference between success and failure. A typical TV commercial shows a salesman who's a flop until his daughter tells him to rinse with Listerine—then he lands the big order. In another, an executive who is slipping tries Micrin, whereupon his boss embraces him and invites him to lunch. Is there any factual basis for these preposterous claims which insult the intelligence of the viewer? I saw none in over three decades in advertising.

It's offensive at any time, and especially at the dinner hour, when commercials for Procter and Gamble's Scope and Johnson and Johnson's Micrin scream the same foul words: "YOU HAVE BAD BREATH!" To top them, along came a multimillion-dollar campaign: "LISTERINE FIGHTS BAD BREATH BEST!" To compound such unproved claims, two different advertisers had their leering announcers follow up unbelievable statements with the ultimate insult: "You know it's true because you can't lie on television."

As the stench of bad-breath advertising fouled the airwaves, Wizard Deodorizer spread the miasma beyond humans with the pronouncement: "YOUR HOUSE HAS BAD BREATH—HOUSE-I-TOSIS!" The bad-breath hurly-burly proved again that there are no limits to bad taste on Madison Avenue.

The shocker headline is a favorite decoy. An ad for St. Joseph Vitamins for Children slammed in letters half an inch high: "STOP VITAMIN SHORTAGE IN CHILDREN." Then in type an eighth-inch high: "A 'balanced' diet can supply all the vitamins your child *normally* needs." The headline's aim is to frighten mothers into feeling that their children have a vitamin shortage—and that St. Joseph Vitamins are a must to combat it.

An inch-high headline: "IS BALDNESS NECESSARY?" The long copy rambles on without a single direct promise or conclusion that baldness is not necessary and can be cured.

Does the advertiser figure that the headline will make men feel that hair *can* be grown on bald heads?

Some ads are amazingly naïve in their deceptions, such as a sign in a store window: "Our adding machines will last a lifetime. Guaranteed for one year."

Significant oversights in advertising copy, intentional or not, are commonplace. A Volkswagen ad showed a car with a crumpled fender. The copy stated that the repair would cost only $24.95 for a new fender plus labor. A VW owner pointed out that the repair of the headlight assembly, also smashed in the photo, would add about another $18.

Much advertising aims to convince by confusing. Ads for Condition by Clairol stated: "Actually makes your hair feel stronger. . . . Revitalizes your hair's inner strength, outer beauty." A dermatologist commented, "This is advertising nonsense. No one could explain 'hair feeling stronger' sensibly because scientifically it's baseless. As for 'revitalizing inner strength,' I don't know what it means, do you?"

Another type of advertising flummery: An ad for Wolfschmidt Vodka, made in the United States, stated: "Odd . . . but true! There is a vodka labeled *genuine* that actually costs less! Its name is Wolfschmidt . . . and it costs only $3.89 a fifth." Asked what is meant by "genuine" vodka, a liquor dealer said, "Well, if it's labeled vodka, I figure it's genuine vodka. Of course if it's gin, it ain't genuine vodka, is it?"

Regarding the ad claim "actually costs less," he reacted dazedly: "At $3.89 a fifth it doesn't cost less than this 'genuine' vodka here at $3.59, or that brand at $3.49. Less than what? Do you figure that ad writer has ever been in a liquor store? One look at the shelves would show him that $3.89 vodka doesn't 'cost less' than $3.49 vodka. Who do those jerks think they're kidding?"

It's illuminating to consider further what an ad does *not* say. A number of makers of different autos and various brands of gasoline all claim to have won first prize in racing and mileage tests; an auto buff explained, "You want to know how they could all win? Easy. The cars and gasolines may be entered in many races. But they only tell in the ads about the ones they won, not those that came out the wrong way for them. A brand may win in one race and lose in six or seven others, but the ads only mention the win."

Weyenberg Shoes ran ads competing with Portage Shoes, and Portage hit at Weyenberg in their ads. For example: "The Weyenberg Shoe Company wishes the Portage Shoe Company lots of luck . . . without going into a whole treatise on the economics of competition, the Portage people have really kept us on our toes. We've had to come to grips with the fact that they make a fine shoe, and that makes us make ours a little finer." What readers were not told is that *both brands are owned by the same corporation.*

Some bank advertising was criticized as "deceptive and misleading" by New York State Superintendent of Banks, Frank Wille. "Banking institutions occupy a special position of trust," he noted. Then he pointed to deceptive ads that emphasize the high interest rate paid on a savings certificate but fail to indicate that the penalty for withdrawing the money before maturity is a loss of much of the interest. Whenever ferocious competition arises, which has happened with banks in an interest war, the penalties for withdrawal are always in small print.

With the exception of savings-bank advertising, it has been noted that any ad headlined "SAVE!" usually has one aim—to make you *spend.*

A common kind of advertising fraud is the use of foreign names on labels of merchandise made in the United States, such as Paris Sportswear made in Hoboken, New Jersey. The FTC had to order one of the biggest manufacturers of men's and women's clothing to stop printing "London" wear large on labels with "Made in U.S.A." in tiny type.

Are testimonials to be believed? A magazine ad for a product that promises a miraculous slimming effect: "Users have made enthusiastic statements like 'Lost thirteen pounds.' . . . 'Lost eighteen pounds.' . . . 'Lost nine pounds.'" Admen know by experience that there are always a few people who are enthusiastic about any product. The big point which testimonials *don't* reveal is how many users were helped, whether most were happy over results, or whether three out of 300,000 were satisfied and 229,997 were disappointed.

Testimonials in general are suspect. Athletes, only one category, have recommended cereals, cigarettes, candy bars, and dozens of other products that they rarely or never use. If an advertiser wants a celebrity testimonial, several services will supply a star who will proclaim publicly, "I love Brand X," or Y or Z—whichever pays the highest. The more the advertiser is willing to shell out, the bigger a celebrity he'll get; there's a $500 list, a $1,000 list, etc. It's that simple and commercial.

Liggett and Myers announced an expenditure of a million dollars to launch a new pipe tobacco, Masterpiece. A color magazine ad featured a photo of Eva Gabor with her dress neckline plunging. It showed her bending toward a can of tobacco and asking: "DARLING, HAVE YOU DISCOVERED MASTERPIECE? THE MOST EXCITING MEN I KNOW ARE SMOKING IT!" Do you think that the most exciting men Eva Gabor knows really smoke Masterpiece?

"JOAN FONTAINE THROWS A SHOT-IN-THE-DARK PARTY AND HER FRIENDS LEARN A THING OR TWO." That's one headline in a celebrity campaign for Fleischmann's Whiskey. The ad pictured "Joan and her friends" sampling shots of whiskey in a room with all lights out, and guessing the brand name, the proof, and the price. Does any adman in his right mind (there are some) think that people reading the ads will throw shot-in-the-dark parties as Fleischmann suggests? No. Then why spend perhaps a million dollars on such a campaign? Only Mad. Ave. could provide a mad-enough answer.

Do most testimonials constitute "fraudulent advertising?" Well, when a movie star poses with a bottle of whiskey and a glass from which he's about to sip with clear delight (I was present), and then says privately, "I'd never touch this cheap poison!"—is that deceitful?

An example of another type of "candid" testimonial: An acquaintance was stopped in a railroad station by a woman who offered him a cup of steaming coffee. She held a microphone and asked, "How did you like it? That's new X-brand instant coffee." The man answered, "I hate every kind of instant coffee. I refuse it at home. Every morning my wife brews a fresh pot of regular coffee and *I love it.*"

The interviewer offered to pay him a sizable sum of money if he signed permission to let them use the tape recording of his remarks in "edited" form. For the money he agreed. Soon his voice was on the air as one of the "candid interviews." In the edited tape he was asked how he liked new X-brand instant coffee. His own voice came through with only the last three words of his original reply: *"I love it."*

Chapter

"LEGITIMATE PUFFERY" OR FRAUD?

5

In a study of "Deceptive Advertising," the *Harvard Law Review* stated: "False advertising . . . lures potential customers away from truthful producers, and injures individual consumers by inducing transactions premised on inaccurate information. . . . Such is the pressure of commercial competition that one false advertisement is likely to breed others in response. . . ."

An angry advertising client complained in a meeting that the competitor was running a campaign headlining that his product was "best." He pounded on the table: "Goddamnit, there are dozens of brands better than his. Ours is twenty times as good. His claim of 'best' is a lie, a fraud on the public—and on us! Why can't we stop him? Why doesn't the government stop him?"

The agencyman said, "Unfortunately such claims are condoned as 'legitimate puffery.'" The fact that the advertising client was using similar unprovable claims was never brought up.

Does "legitimate puffery" add up to deception? *The New Yorker* magazine refuses what it considers undesirable advertising, yet in one issue, each of three different ads for bourbon claimed its brand was the best: "JIM BEAM—THE WORLD'S FINEST BOURBON." "WILD TURKEY BOURBON—THERE IS ALWAYS ONE BEST." "WALKER'S BOURBON—NOTHING ELSE QUITE MEASURES UP." Another bourbon campaign: "OLD TAYLOR—THE BEST AMERICA HAS TO OFFER."

In other brands, one competitor after another in wines, Scotches, gins, and brandies, claims to be "best." Hundreds of other advertisers in other fields—detergents, foods, drugs, cosmetics, and so on, advertise that they're "best." We have become so accustomed to this "legitimate puffery" that we hardly recognize the claim of "best" as a lie.

An ad featured: "CLAN MACGREGOR RARE SCOTCH—ONLY $4.99 FOR 4/5TH QUART. IT'S LIGHT AND SMOOTH. TRULY, THERE'S NONE BETTER!" In tiny type the ad also stated: "Eighty proof." Most costly Scotches are 86 proof or more, and aged Scotches cost far more. Whiskeys, wines, etc., are a matter of taste—and of the buyer's pocketbook. "Best" is at best a vague claim that is not and cannot be substantiated.

E. Martin Brandy at $5.29 per four-fifths quart was advertised as "There's none better," although there are hundreds of brandies (including aged cognac) which experts would call far superior. A letter from an advertising agency executive to the advertising director of a newspaper running that campaign stated: "A woman has questioned me, 'When the advertiser of a cheap product, in a field where there are many costlier and clearly superior brands, advertises that 'There's none better' (not 'none better at this price'), the newspaper and every adman know it's a lie. Why then is such advertising produced and run?' Can you provide the answer, from your responsibility as publisher of the ad?"

The reply from the newspaper admanager contained no explanation, only excuses, and concluded unhappily: "I don't think I've helped much." The newspaper continued to accept the questionable ads.

A visitor to the home of a liquor man who advertises his brand as "best" said, "Your brand sells for under five dollars. The whiskey you're pouring costs over eight dollars. Isn't it better than your 'best' brand?"

The host frowned as he poured. "Sure, what's the difference? Our ad is simply 'legitimate puffery.' "

"Legitimate puffery—or a lie?"

The advertiser shrugged. "Okay, I suppose it's a lie—but it doesn't hurt anybody."

"Your son Johnny seems like a fine youngster," the guest went on. "Suppose you caught him in a lie and said, 'Johnny, you're lying.' And he answered, 'So what, Dad, it doesn't hurt anybody. . . .' "

The guest later asked me, as an advertising executive, "If the force of over $17 billion of advertising expenditure a year approves self-serving lies as permissible lies, how does that affect the nation's ethics, the moral standards of children and adults?"

The obvious answer is a hard one for admen to swallow.

One wonders whether most liquor advertising is written before or after the product has been imbibed. Ballantine Beer advertised, "Won't fill you up, won't let you down . . . hey, friend, do it again!" The truth is, of course, that if you drink enough of any beer it's bound to let you down under the nearest table. Schaefer's, which like other beer companies professes to promote temperate drinking, hammers: "Schaefer is the one beer to have when you're having more than one" and it won't bloat you "beer after beer after beer." Following up this incitement to drink more, Rheingold echoed, "There's always room for more."

Beer companies contend also that they try not to direct their advertising at youngsters. Nevertheless, baseball broadcasts in many cities are dominated by beer sponsors; children form a very large portion of the audiences. In a flagrant instance Country Club Malt Liquor, twice as strong as beer, placed their ads on rock-and-roll radio programs and on a TV show of folk music with primarily teen-age audiences. Their trade publicity affirmed that they were aiming their promotion at "the young swinger."

What is the main reason for such fakery and the big brag that "we're best"? It pleases the advertiser's vanity to see and hear his products proclaimed as "best," even though he's paying for the empty self-praise. Furthermore, agencies find that such back-patting is an easy, lazy way to 1. get an approval, and 2. avoid risk of displeasing the client. Finally, many admen are convinced that if they keep stressing "best," the public will believe it even if it's patently untrue.

On the contrary, it has been proven often that it's not only honest but also profitable to make a specific believable statement rather than an unprovable boast. If Goodyear advertised (which it does not) "Goodyear tires are best," it would have little effect other than to antagonize many prospects. Instead, Goodyear advertising states: "More people ride on Goodyear than any other kind." This is specific, factual, and impressive. It gets across the point that people wouldn't keep coming back for more Goodyear tires if dissatisfied with their quality.

Is misrepresentation any less deceitful when it cloaks unprovable claims in the guise of gags? The advertiser's alibi is, "We were only kidding. Where's your sense of humor?" A commercial for frozen orange juice shows a caveman trying to smash an orange into juice with a stone sledgehammer, then beaming as he discovers the small can of frozen juice. The announcer calls the brand "the greatest advance in orange juice in twenty million years." When asked about the "great advance," a wholesale grocer said, "The only really new thing about this 'new' product . . . is the commercial. If it fools people into buying more of the brand I'll sell more. I'm in business for a profit. I'm no Diogenes looking for an honest advertiser. I gave up and blew out my lamp long ago."

When a company's advertising gives you the impression that *only* its product contains a special miracle ingredient, it ain't necessarily so. It may be just another common form of the permissible lie. Shell spent many millions of dollars year after year advertising that Platformate put more mileage into every gallon of its gasoline. The impression given to all car owners I questioned was that this feature was *exclusive* to Shell. Not so!

Investigation has proved that "Platformate or its equivalent is present in virtually every gasoline refined." Commercials showed that Shell gasoline with Platformate provided more mileage than gasoline without Platformate. But gasoline without Platformate is an inferior product, not any leading brand. A competitor in West Germany said that Shell's saying, "Our gasoline contains Platformate" is like a baker advertising, "I bake my cake with flour."

Shell spokesmen replied, "That same comment could be made about most good advertising of most products. All our campaign is saying is that Super Shell is designed to give you good mileage. . . . Of course, Platformate is nothing new. . . . We have never claimed that Platformate was an exclusive ingredient."

We all have been conned by the misuse of quotations from a review into seeing a show or a movie, or buying a book. Critic Howard Taubman turned thumbs down emphatically on the play *Ben Franklin in Paris*. He praised only the star's performance. However, the day after, a full-page ad appeared in *The New York Times* in the same drama section where the unfavorable review had run. Big black type proclaimed: "ROBERT PRESTON IN BIG FAT MUSICAL HIT . . . Taubman, *N.Y. Times*. . . . Robert Preston . . . a beguiling companion on any stage. If anybody can charm the French court into granting recognition to a new nation, Mr. Preston can. Mr. Preston's rapier way with a wisecrack is very much of our time and our theater." Actually, Taubman had written *against* the wisecrack, claiming that it gave "so much contemporary snap that the spirit of '76 [was] instantly dispelled."

A full-page ad in *The New York Times* for the musical play *Illya Darling* quoted Edwin Newman, critic for the National Broadcasting Company, as saying: "Melina [the star] is *irresistible*." Mr. Newman had actually said: "*Illya Darling* rests on the premise that Melina Mercouri is irresistible. Even if one accepts this unlikely premise, this is a tasteless, heavy-handed show beyond anyone's capacity to bring to life."

Resenting the quote in the ad, Mr. Newman later stated in a telecast: "I did not like *Illya Darling* and I consider Melina Mercouri eminently resistible." The advertiser alibied that the "regrettable error was caused by the heat of an advertising deadline" and that there had been "no intent to deceive."

Many movie ads select one word or two of praise from hundreds in a damning review. An ad in *The New York Times* for *The Pumpkin Eater* read: "STRIKING EFFECTS! Anne Bancroft measured and moody . . . for this role she was voted best actress at the Cannes Film Festival. . . . Bosley Crowther, *N.Y. Times*." The phrase "striking effects" came from these lines: "Mr. Clayton's direction [referred to earlier as "photographic fidgets"] is somewhat mechanical, too, tumbling his drama in a confusion of jump cuts and fleeting images. The cutting style is distracting, but some [here it comes] striking effects are achieved."

Regarding the performance of Anne Bancroft, generally a superb actress, Crowther wrote: "She wallows in self-pity and philoprogenitiveness. She presents a tiresome woman, impressed more than we are with her woes. For this she was voted the best actress at the Cannes Film Festival." The critic's sarcasm about the vote for best actress was turned into a compliment.

The adman says, "It's legitimate puffery. It doesn't hurt anybody." It defrauds people into spending their dollars by twisting an unfavorable review into an enthusiastic recommendation.

Year after year movie advertisers have promised to clean up advertising practices involving use of misleading quotes, and also the suggestive advertising of exaggerated sexuality. Year after year the practice continues. Here are four ads from *The New York Times* movie section, appearing the same day:

"*Where Love Has Gone*. It's gone WRONG! It's gone WILD!" The illustration shows a man stripped to the waist biting a woman's neck. She is dressed in a slip.

Different ad, same scene, but the man isn't biting the woman's neck, he's pulling down the shoulder strap of her black slip. "*Youngblood Hawke*. All the blister-heat of the best seller! A woman could feel him across a room. . . ."

Third ad, the man is slapping a woman who is wearing a nightgown. She's pulling down the top herself to bare a shoulder. "*Kitten with a Whip*. She's what they call a real smoky kitten . . . the kicks she digs . . . the swingers she runs with and the guy she hooked her claws into. . . ."

In the fourth ad, both man and woman are stripped as far as is visible. He's either kissing or biting her neck—the back of his head blocks part of the view. "*Woman in the Dunes* . . . a strong emanation of passion surges from the screen!"

A later film ad: "Some movie ads tend to exaggerate. We wouldn't want to do that. We don't have to. This one will speak for itself." The movie: *The Family Way.* The large illustration showed a couple in nightdress sitting on a bed, starting to make love.

The point here doesn't concern censorship. It illuminates the common practice of advertisers who deny deception and then repeatedly commit infractions for their own gain, regardless of the public interest. That's show business—and most every other kind of business. The pitchman has always operated according to W. C. Fields' motto: "Never give a sucker an even break."

Those who count on admen to discipline themselves are living in a dream world. Paul Rand Dixon, chairman of the FTC, speaking to a conference of advertising executives, said: "It has become all too apparent that wolves are not led onto paths of righteousness by offering them the carrot of self-discipline. Wolves ignore carrots; they want meat, and they don't care how bloody it is."

Chapter

THE WAR AGAINST GOVERNMENT REGULATION

6

"I regret to announce," a chairman tells his board of directors in a cartoon, "that despite governmental interference in business and a never-ending snarl of bureaucratic red tape, our corporation has the highest net income in its history."

Madison Avenue as a whole hates government. Sometimes cooler heads try to conceal this. Thomas B. Adams, outgoing chairman of the American Association of Advertising Agencies (the Four A's), advised in his farewell address: "Government is big. It is getting bigger. And since, in many important instances, we cannot go it alone, we had better learn to live with it. . . . The Government is here to stay and so are we."

A week earlier, Jerry Della Femina, vice president of Ted Bates and Company, had told another industry audience: "Advertising is being clubbed [by government]. The business of business is being clubbed. And the only thing to do when you're being clubbed is to club back. No, I don't want to communicate with those people who want to kill advertising. I'd prefer to be part of the movement to destroy those people who want to kill advertising." He referred to government representatives as "nincompoops . . . ridiculous . . . harebrained."

Archibald McG. Foster, head of Bates, quickly announced that Mr. Della Femina's inflammatory views were strictly his own and didn't represent those of the agency. Foster also warned his organization that all speeches should be cleared beforehand with agency top management: "We have a philosophy and a point of view. . . . Our corporate voice must be a consistent one." (Several months later, Bates and Mr. Della Femina parted company.)

Inside Madison Avenue, the anti-government attitude expressed by Mr. Della Femina is the prevalent one. The apparent cooperation with government is usually only a false face. A sincere approach of cooperation to build mutual trust would help business, government, and the public. Such trust must be backed by honesty in advertising. In my experience, the fear of government regulation and interference usually stems from promoting the permissible or blatant lie, or other reprehensible practices.

The chief government body regulating truth in advertising is the Federal Trade Commission. In spite of the overwhelming evidence of much deception, many admen insist that you can't get away with fakery today because the FTC will expose any fraud. This is outright hypocrisy, aimed at deluding the public. Advertisers have many special methods for "getting away with murder" under the present operations of the FTC.

Because of the tremendous amount of advertising to be checked, and the relatively small staff allotted to the FTC, an enormous volume of questionable ads gets by. The agency and advertising client know that most campaigns, no matter how misleading, can run at least a year or two, usually more, before an order comes from the FTC to stop the advertising and to promise not to continue it. The FTC has no real power to punish.

"Effective policing of the multibillion dollar advertising industry," the *Harvard Law Review* stated, "cannot be expected from an agency with restricted budget and manpower, whose sole formal method of proceeding is on a case-by-case basis, and whose initial sanction is an order that the respondent 'go and sin no more.' "

Therefore Madison Avenue frequently takes this course of action with respect to FTC regulations: The advertiser and agency agree on a specific campaign. They know that some of the claims are unfounded and misleading, or—in Mad-avenese—*iffy*. That means the admen know they can't defend the claims if challenged by the FTC.

Nonetheless the agency proceeds with the campaigns, presenting the misleading copy on TV, in magazines, or wherever the ads may appear. Why do the agency and client take the risk of running ads which they know can get them in trouble? The answer is simple: The advertiser believes that by making his extravagant claim, his permissible lie, he'll get lots more people to try his product. He knows that chances are he'll get a year or two of extra sales power before the FTC jumps on him. Perhaps the FTC may never get around to him, since they're so understaffed and overloaded with cases.

He knows, too, that by the time the FTC orders him to stop using this particular claim, he will probably have switched to some other theme which would require a whole new round of investigation.

He can say to the FTC, "We did no wrong. However, there's no point in fighting you—we've already stopped using that claim." If he feels that the campaign is almost worn out, he can protest his ignorance and give in with, "Okay, we'll cease and desist."

Patent medicine claims and medical "cures" are as old as time, and continue today. *Advertising Age* reported these typical facts:

> The Federal Trade Commission has ordered National Research Corporation, Lafayette, Louisiana, to stop making false therapeutic claims for Enurol, and to drop the word "research" from its name. The word "research" is deceptive, FTC said, because the company is not engaged in scientific or any other kind of research. The one person responsible for research terminated his education at the high school level, FTC said, and has never taken courses in chemistry, nutrition, biology or other scientific fields.

The report further noted a cease-and-desist order on these claims: "That Enurol prevents, treats, relieves or cures arthritis and other degenerative diseases; will decrease the cholesterol in the body; will enable a person to maintain good health; will help rid the body of damaged tissues; and is a new or scientific discovery or achievement."

How is an advertiser usually punished if found guilty? He promises he'll drop the claim and be good. There is no other punishment. He then sets about finding a new way to advertise with amended or different claims which may be more acceptable to the FTC and yet promising enough to lure purchasers—with little or no change in the product.

In a few flagrant cases of fraud, the FTC may stop the advertiser in a hurry, particularly if many complaints are received. These are often originated by competitors. Sometimes the Food and Drug Administration is involved, and this government body has the power to seek fines, as occurred in the Regimen case described earlier.

Of course every advertising campaign cannot be double-checked by anyone, including the FTC. At best, the commission tries to eliminate the most flagrant advertising claims within a year or two after the campaign has started. In the inner offices the adman complains, "Imagine those stupid FTC bastards jumping on us for a campaign we stopped using a year ago!" The same indignant reactions to some of the exposures in this book will be heard on Madison Avenue: "We no longer run the stuff Baker is criticizing." But while the words may have been changed, the *intent* of the new campaign can probably be counted upon to deceive the buying public.

Another method of getting around the FTC is to promise not to run any more advertising or print anything more that promotes the claims in question—but that's a big loophole. The advertiser is generally permitted to "use up" display material he has already completed which contains the questionable statements. He has a good deal of such material in warehouses and in stores. As he "uses it up," the extravagant claims are exposed to the public for a long, long time after the cease-and-desist order has been in effect, sometimes *years* longer.

If called to account, the advertiser says, "It's not my fault.

I can't stop stores from using the display material." He adds, "I'll do my best to check the stores." Frequently the best he does is to stall until the displays have been worn out in the natural course of business.

There are, of course, cases where honest advertisers have felt that their claims were justified but have acceded to an adverse FTC ruling in order to avoid time-consuming wrangling. Others fight back at FTC accusations, and in some instances have won in the courts. In such cases they had been subjected to unfavorable publicity and considerable expense, and they protested accordingly. The damage they suffer is unfair to them but is due to the infractions of so many other companies.

In the vast majority of accusations by the FTC, the advertiser signs the "stop" order because he knows that his claims and promises are indefensible. Those who scream the loudest about "government persecution" are often the greatest offenders. As soon as the fuss has died down they're right back to advertising their products with other "iffy" copy. Every adman knows that if the FTC were to prosecute every advertiser whose ads contain something deceitful or misleading, the commission would need hundreds more investigators, lawyers, courtrooms, and judges.

When I showed these pages about the FTC to an agency friend, he shook his head, frowned, and said, "Brrr! Do you think all this should be revealed?"

"Is it true?"

"Ye-es."

"Insiders know it's true?"

"Yes, but—"

"The FTC knows it's so?"

"Of course, yet—"

"Then the public should know about it."

He did not agree.

Chapter

FRAUDULENT . . . OR JUST PLAIN SILLY?

7

The following ad filled one third of a *Good Housekeeping* magazine page: "Time to consult your bun-eez horoscope for news of size-pruf holeproof and truly whymsy hy-test quality panties. If you are feminine sissy britches or imps sport-eez at heart your best bet in sportswear, twinklette playwear, strutwear is found in the fashion names of nolde and golden nolde." The ad bore a large *Good Housekeeping* seal.

Since "many of my best friends are admen," I've become involved in bitter arguments when attacking some advertising approaches as deceptive. A frequent reaction: "Advertising fraudulent? No! Just plain silly? Well, maybe. . . ." The latter always referred to the competitor's efforts.

"Silly" advertising is well defined by David Ogilvy as "flatulent puffery." According to Webster, "flatulent" means: "1. Of or having gas in the stomach or intestines. 2. Producing gas in the stomach or intestines, as certain foods [for thought?]. 3. Windy or empty in speech; vain; pompous; pretentious." It all fits the asinine in advertising.

Here are a few examples from the overwhelming mass of ads exuding the offensive odor of "flatulent puffery." It's almost impossible to believe that otherwise level-headed businessmen spend millions of dollars on so many nonsensical ads.

Advertising spokesmen proclaim in speeches that it's an outmoded concept to consider that the general public has an average twelve-year-old mentality. Countless ads still confirm the "outmoded concept." A twelve-year-old friend of mine asserts that most ads, especially TV commercials, are created to appeal to those far below his mental level.

You would think that admen and advertisers, rereading the fantastic (using this much-abused word advisedly) copy quoted here would feel embarrassment, possibly even shame. You might even hope they would think twice before releasing similar nonsense in future ads. I wouldn't bet on it. Admen are too much in love with their own words and ideas to amend their approach. Furthermore, it's almost impossible for an adman to confess, "I goofed." That's especially true of agencymen within client's ear range.

Admen frequently talk to themselves in ads, in a language comprehensible only to themselves: "Evan-Piconery! Is to wonderful in. Whimsy in. Very appeal to him in. These sweater wonderfuls. . . ." Another: "Is to poor little boy sweater in. More of a great big girl in. . . . These pure wool poors. . . ."

Another candidate for Silliest Ad of the Decade: "LIKABLE, BEAUTIFUL BUICK. AFFORDABLE AND REACHABLE. SMACK IN WALLET RANGE." The car was shown at an angle that you could see in a showroom if you got down on the floor on your hands and knees and looked up. Our local Buick salesman commented, "Those ad guys are nuts. They sure don't know anything about cars or people."

Quaker Oats spent about $85,000 for a two-page spread in *Life* magazine and hundreds of thousands of dollars elsewhere to state: "MAMA, MAKE THEM [the kids] LAUGH. TELL THEM QUAKER OATS IS KIND OF A LOVE-PAT FOR TUMMIES." Even an adman would be nauseated to hear his wife tell his youngsters at breakfast, "Eat your Quaker Oats, it's a love-pat for tummies."

A Green Giant Corn ad conveyed this homily: "The world liked this corn very much—even Uncle Augbert liked it. And now the Green Giant has a well-worn path to his door. Which is nice because he does like people." Feeling a little green? Leo Burnett, head of the agency which prepared the ad, once said, "I am one who believes that one of the greatest dangers of advertising is not that of misleading people, but that of boring them to death."

A Celanese ad showed a pretty pop singer surrounded by chefs: "SINGER LESLIE UGGAMS MAKES GREAT LASAGNE." The ad has her tell at length how she makes lasagne, how it helps her "unwind." "She laughed. 'I go to small Italian restaurants [when too busy to cook lasagne] and eat other people's lasagne.'" Is the ad selling Leslie's Celanese Lasagne? No. "For this [eating lasagne] we have the perfect dress. . . ." Surprise—it's made out of a Celanese fabric, not lasagne.

A Philadelphia Carpet Company ad featured carpeting in "Tintinnabulating bell tones . . . twelve colors that stir, soothe, set the spirits soaring and chime as melodically as a carillon . . . inspired by Edgar Allan Poe's noble poem, 'The Bells.'" People I queried said they prefer a carpet that just lays there quietly without pealing. The rattling sound you hear now is Edgar Allan Poe turning over in his grave.

An Armstrong Vinyl ad showed a woman fencing fiercely on a vinyl floor: "ANY MAN (*swish!*) WHO RENEGES (*swish! swish!*) ON HIS PROMISE (*swish!*) TO BUY HIS WIFE (*swish! swish! swish!*) A MONTINA VINYL CORLON FLOOR (*swish!*) IS IN FOR BIG TROUBLE (*touché*)." The headline combined eight "swishes!" and one "touché"—a new record.

Does No-Cal tell you right out that its quinine water is the one with no calories and helps you control your weight? No. Their ad pictured a shivering man saying, "This is the t-t-tonic with the colder t-t-touch. There's no sugar, no c-c-calories to heat you up! Strictly a chilling jolt of authentic tonic f-f-flavor! Even the price keeps you cooler under the c-c-collar!" Why all this c-c-confusion? To impress the c-c-client with the agency's c-c-cleverness.

Are such examples of "silly copy" in print or on the air the exception? Are they effective? Stockton Helffrich of the National Association of Broadcasters commented in a speech to admen: "Experience in my office reveals a steady flow of copy which borders on the ridiculous and which common sense viewers cannot identify with or believe in. They shrug it off as being typical nonsense fed their way in return for the program. But purchase and use of products should result in consumer confirmation of the advertising message. Anything less results in built-up, long-range resentment from the public, damaging to advertisers and media alike."

Women are continuously assaulted with cosmetic copy such as: "Revlon Ultima II non-makeup makeup . . . transparesscent . . . souffléd texture . . . spins out a complexion like a sweep of silk . . . sweeps across your cheeks like an unexpected compliment . . . the perfect fraud . . . as though this were not makeup at all but something fed to you on a silver spoon."

A woman reading this winced and said, "I think I get it. This 'transparesscent, souffléd' goo looks like makeup but you don't smear it on, you eat it."

Another cosmetic excrescence: "With Avon Rapture [fragrance] you feel happily free but captivating—for Rapture is sensitive to you. . . . Rapture has beautiful hopes for you." Avon sells through home representatives. One of them looked disgusted upon reading this ad and remarked, "Imagine me sitting in any living room and telling a woman, 'Rapture has beautiful hopes for you.' Isn't an ad supposed to speak person-to-person? If I talked that way to my customers they'd think I just escaped from a mental hospital."

The slogan of Riker's Counter Luncheonettes in New York City: "No finer food at any price." The same ownership runs The Four Seasons, The Forum of the Twelve Caesars, and other restaurants where dinner checks can easily run to $25 or more per person. Is the slogan then based on the conviction that people will believe anything—or is it just plain foolishness? Or is the $25 dinner check at The Four Seasons a gyp since they can't serve finer food than Riker's at a dollar or two—according to their own slogan?

A Madison Avenue stereotype is the preposterous Big Brag ad: "Open up the White Rock and live! White Rock creates a light-hearted atmosphere that makes everyone feel in-tune, ready for a good time. Your party is off to a lively start and lively is the way it will stay until the last goodnight is said.

. . . Stamp out dull parties . . . pour fun-filled White Rock!"

A wine advertiser warned: "IT CAN'T BE GAY WITHOUT CHAUVENET RED CAP." If such advertisers' own parties depend for success on the brand of soda or wine they serve, heaven help their guests. Another advertiser took advantage of the current advertising silliness with the headline: "WILL THIS CLUB SODA MAKE YOU THE PERFECT HOST? CANADA DRY SAYS NO."

A slogan has been defined as "a good old American substitute for the facts." The value of a slogan is generally overrated. One problem is that the repeated slogan may not fit the rest of the ad copy as conditions change. Kelly's Print Shop in Columbia, Missouri, found this out with their slogan, "Kelly Did It." They imprinted it in small type somewhere on every piece of their output. Objections developed when they printed the slogan on birth announcements.

An ex-adwoman, founder of Switzerland's English-language newspaper the *Weekly Tribune*, Mrs. Casey I. Herrick, attacked "Sloppy Copy" in an article in *Printers' Ink* magazine:

> In a single half hour of browsing through magazines I found more than a dozen ads claiming that their products were smoother; longer-lasting; cheaper; better; washed whiter; stayed fresh longer. Admiral TV lasts longer and works better. Mani Magic removes cuticles three times faster (than that pair of scissors my son used to cut his hair with, no doubt).
>
> Are we really such suckers that we swallow those pointless hooks? I doubt it—and I think the public is being cheated by the manufacturers if there is nothing more to be said about their products, or the manufacturers are being taken by their agencies if this is the best copy they can turn out.

Magazines spill over with examples of "sloppy copy": "Durene is the miracle cotton yarn that makes clothes wash cleaner, look brighter, feel more comfortable, and wear far longer." Than *what*? The finish: ". . . nothing stays as new as Durene." Said a puzzled woman, "I guess it means I should buy 'nothing' because it 'stays as new as Durene.' "

Another embarrassing blast: "Among all the wonderful Italian things America has discovered, nothing is more so than Fiat's 1100D Sedan! That includes the wine, the women, the music, the art—even great, historic Roma." A traveler to Italy and an admirer of Sophia Loren commented, "After that absurd claim, how can I believe anything said in favor of Fiat?"

An ad for Contadina Tomato Paste, a division of the giant Carnation Company, showed a tintype-style photo of an old-fashioned Italian lady: "Mama cried when we took the Bay of Naples off the Contadina can. Mama was born in Naples. Nobody can explain to her why the picture of the Bay had to go off the Contadina can when we began to make our Tomato Paste in California."

A neighbor envisioned dear old Mama bending over a hot kitchen stove and cooking and crying (all the way to the bank) into millions of cans of tomato paste while she paid about $50,000 for this page in *Life* magazine. She said, "It enrages me that the advertiser considers me so stupid. It's a sure way to keep Contadina out of *my* kitchen."

An ad for Rolex watches featured a photo of A & P multimillionaire Huntington Hartford and Edouard Cournand with this copy: " 'Where did you get your Rolex?' Mr. Cournand asked Mr. Hartford. You might think that's a pretty silly way to start a conversation." "Yes," a noted engineer friend remarked, "and a pretty silly way to try to sell thousand-dollar watches to adults who can afford that price."

This full-page ad for *Look*, a publication noted for clear illuminating editorial matter, appeared in *The New Yorker* and other magazines:

> "Views make news.
> News makes views.
> *Look* views news.
> Views views.
> Makes news.
> Makes LOOK."

How does the asininity come about? Such nonsense ads commonly grow from constant, desperate pressure on agencymen from advertising clients to be different, original, and creative. Often dozens of writers and artists are put to work in an agency in a frenzied rush to produce "genius ideas." This habitually occurs when product sales are dipping or if the client is dissatisfied with the current advertising.

"Press the panic button!" is the cry at the agency. Meetings are called and disbanded. Harried writers and artists work night after night. Everything is tabbed "Rush! Rush! Rush!" The craziest ideas are created, rejected, revised, accepted, twisted, bulled through in a kind of mass hysteria. Ads erupt in a chaotic fury in which neither the agencymen nor the client group can finally see straight or think clearly. When the dust clears and the blood has been mopped up, the campaign has been approved at last for better or worse—invariably worse.

Later the client is likely to scream after watching the resultant commercials on his TV set at home, "My God, how the hell did that ever get by—who approved that? Get that ridiculous stuff off the air—as of now!" More often, no one at either the agency or advertiser's office sees the commercials objectively—ever. TV viewers suffer accordingly, and so do product sales.

Researcher Eric Marder has stated that based on the results of a series of studies, "Occasionally we've had to tell a client, 'It would have paid you to pay someone *not* to run this ad.' "

Chapter

FUNNY ADS? OR PHONY?

8

The high irritation quotient of advertising bothers most people even more than the fakery. Most commercials meant to be funny usually wind up as phony. When Bob Hope, sponsored by Chrysler, says, "Next week we celebrate the landing of the Pilgrims on Chrysler Rock." Adding, "I may not be accurate but I sure am commercial," we are amused—the first time. The trouble with humorous commercials on TV is that admen won't recognize that even the brightest joke or sequence wears out quickly with repetition. After the third hearing, the "funny" commercial arouses annoyance and antagonism.

The exclamation point (the main "talent" of many a copywriter) has been described as "a period that has blown its top." Humor in advertising usually blows its top trying too hard, going too far, repeating too often. Here is a typically witless cartoon ad: "When she said she was an old-fashioned girl, I quickly added liquor to Holland House Old-Fashioned Mix and had it made. The Old Fashioned that is. It was sensational. It would do a great bartender proud. The Old Fashioned that is." Apparently even the client decided that the ad was ineffectual as well as unfunny; he switched agencies.

A page in *The New Yorker* for Andrew Geller Shoes parodies a child's reader with its repetitious "This is Spot [a dog]. THIS IS SPAT [a shoe]. Spat is a Gamin. Gamin Gamin Spat. See Spat go. Go go Spat."

In the same magazine another page ad read: "A FRANK

REPLY TO THOSE WHO THINK THE REAL MACKENZIE SCOTCH FOR SCOTCH-MEN SOCIETY ARE A BUNCH OF SCOTCH SCOTCH. Oh, what bickering brattle they would prattle about such a doughty cause as ours. And don't they hae all the gall, calling the RMSFSS a bunch of skinflints in Scotsmen's clothing when all the time they're after giving us a fleecing by shipping The Real MACKENZIE down the river to America!"

MacKenzie paid thousands of dollars to estrange Scotch drinkers with that copywriter's nightmare. There's more meaning in lines by the double-talk comedian Al Kelly who told audiences earnestly, "I think the real problem here is to forsook the nikker on the helve." After a talk at a dinner honoring the Supreme Court, one justice told Kelly, "If ever a man belonged in Washington, you do." And on Madison Avenue.

Straining to be clever, Frigidaire doesn't make dishwashers any more—they advertise Custom-Imperial Super-Surge Dishmobiles. A dishmobile doesn't wash dishes, it "sanitizes" them. General Motors decided that used Cadillacs are not used cars—they dubbed them "cars with previous service."

Nor is religion beyond the reach of the adman. A radio jingle for United Presbyterian Church is attributed to comedy-writer Stan Freberg, who was once quoted as saying, "Advertising doesn't have to be dull, insipid, nauseating." His religious jingle:

> "Doesn't it get a little lonely sometimes
> Out on that limb without Him?
> . . . Why try and go it alone?
> The blessings you lose may be your own."

Another example of Madison Avenue genius applied to religion is this poster in a Pennsylvania shopping center: "Worship God in Your Car—Casually Dressed—Comfortably Seated—Valley Forge Drive-In Theatre."

The eternal triangle has finally gone commercial: "THIS IS A LOVE AFFAIR BETWEEN HIM AND HER . . . AND A SKYLARK." Pontiac headlined: "FOR PEOPLE WHO LOVE CARS—A

CAR THAT LOVES PEOPLE." The ad also referred to the car as "one of the winningest influencers."

How is this for being tone-deaf to words? Green Mint Mouthwash offered "DOUBLE YOUR MONEY BACK IF YOU DON'T FEEL THE GREEN TASTE OF CONFIDENCE." Do you want a "green taste of confidence" in your mouth?

Madison Avenue loves coy copy such as this Rice Council ad: "A hurrah-type switch from you-know-what on the dinner plate. Parsley Rice! . . . or rice easy-fixed lots of other flavor-full ways . . . it's clean-grown in the USA." Translation: Parsley Rice is a delicious change from potatoes, and easy to make. Why doesn't the ad say so? Because the agency tried to create what the Rice Council might call "clever advertising," rather than talk naturally to women who buy food for the family. Imagine a wife telling her husband at dinner, "Here, darling, is a hurrah-type switch from you-know-what—and it's clean-grown in the USA." He'd head for the nearest saloon.

How do silly, soggy, double-talk ads come into being? I attended an actual meeting in the office of the advertising head of a large food product manufacturer. He phoned the agency first thing in the morning: "I had an inspiration last night. Our TV commercial problem is solved. Come and get it!"

We hurried over to hear him explain: "I had a dream last night about our cheese spread. In it this little guy in a court jester's costume, wearing a big handlebar mustache, knocks at the door of a fancy castle. A butler lets him in. The comical jester pulls our package out from under his cloak. Funny, eh? There's a lot of hilarious talk between the two in broad English dialect—that's for 'class'—all about our cheese. Finally the butler tastes a little on his finger and he runs to tell his 'Marster' that he's found the most wonderful spread in the world."

He sat back. "I'd like to see some words and sketches for a sixty-second cartoon commercial like that and other funny ones using the same comical little jester with the handlebar mustache. He'll sell our stuff like no other commercials ever did before."

While the usual yes-men were congratulating the client, the bug-eyed TV creative director sitting next to me whispered, "He's got to be kidding. No?" "No." Aloud he ventured a cautious, "Uh—do you think that commercial has any flavor appeal?"

The client's advertising head hotly defended his cheese dream. "It's got a helluva lot more socko than those stinkin' dull commercials we're running showing a family being served our stuff at their dinner table like every other goddamned food product. At least people will look at these clever cartoon commercials and *remember our name!*"

The commercials he insisted on were designed and produced at a cost of about $50,000. They ran in a "saturation campaign" in several cities as a test. "Saturation" involves loading in the commercials and bombarding the audience with dozens of blurbs each week for a short period. Maybe people were intrigued by the comical little jester and remembered the product name. They certainly didn't buy the product. Sales dipped and then gently expired. As usual, instead of firing the admanager, the client fired the agency.

The backlash of these silly ads is the waste of millions, and the agencies and advertisers are sabotaged by their own fatuity and self-indulgence. People, just plain people who buy products, don't know what the ads are trying to say—and they care less. The public doesn't clamor for advertising clarity because they're not that concerned. The advertiser has wasted his dollars in a frivolous, profitless spasm. He hasn't made any meaningful contact with you, the potential buyer. Everyone is a loser.

Test after test proves that the silly ads (not the few that are genuinely humorous) rarely pay off. One test compared two ads for Schick Electric Shaver Centers. The purpose was to get more men to bring in their shavers for overhaul and tune-up. One ad had the cutie-pie headline: "IT'S SPRING . . . AND TIME TO HAVE YOUR HEAD EXAMINED." The other test ad asked straight out: "HOW MUCH SHOULD IT COST TO GET AN ELECTRIC SHAVER FIXED?"

Almost twice as many men noted the straightforward headline; five times as many men read most of the ad that provided information rather than the wisecrack heading.

National Biscuit Company introduced a cookie with the coy name of Snickerdoodles. According to Howard W. Wilson, director of marketing, Snickerdoodles flopped "miserably." Nabisco tried a new name which clicked. In no time sales zoomed past $4 million. The name that attracted shoppers was Cinnamon Sugar Cookies.

Then why does the silly syndrome exist? It's due primarily to "creative people" in advertising trying to impress the agency bosses, the client, and other admen with their cleverness. It's not so much "the public be damned" as the conviction expressed by an agency executive: "I don't give a damn about pleasing anybody but the guy who pays our agency bills. He likes this corny stuff and we give it to him." On the other side, advertising clients often contend, "The agency convinced us that this far-out stuff would sell. It didn't. Our loss, their funeral."

A good many people in advertising, especially at the creative end, are frustrated "artists" of typewriter and brush. They relieve their frustrations by making cute ads that put more emphasis on being different than on productive meaning.

Hopefully admen reading this will think twice before they write, aiming to create more helpful, informative ads instead of concentrating on phony blasts. These are the boys who are more concerned with "Look how good I am," instead of "Here's how the product is good for you."

There's a big difference between writing ads and writing articles for magazines. Most magazine editors want articles that inform, interest, entertain, inspire, and serve readers. The agencyman is primarily concerned with pleasing the advertising client. The result is too frequently a razzle-dazzle approach which tries to fool the customer into reading or listening to the ad in hopes that he'll buy the product.

The stream of funny/phony ads gurgles on endlessly:

"RONRICO'S NOT AN OLD-TIME MOVIE STAR. RONRICO'S A RUM." Is that any reason to buy this brand of rum? Next question, please.

"THERE'S SOMETHING ABOUT WEEJUNS THAT SAYS SOMETHING ABOUT YOU. BASS WEEJUN MOCCASINS ARE A WAY OF LIFE. . . ."

Silliness extends from head to toe: "THE KNOX TWENTY [hat]—AN EXERCISE IN VIGOROUS ELEGANCE. . . ." "QUINSANA [powder] PRESENTS THE JOLLY FOOT. . . ."

Said Jean Wade Rindlaub, former vice president of Batten, Barton, Durstine and Osborn, after her eye-opening retirement: ". . . it is indeed like looking for the proverbial needle in a haystack or a contact lens in a swimming pool to collect a good sampling of straight, honest advertisements."

Novelist Ralph Ellison has said: "It is the job of the writer to make the inarticulate intelligent." From the evidence, the aim of many adwriters is far too often to make the intelligent inarticulate.

Chapter 9

HOW IMITATION BUILDS IRRITATION

"The advertising business is made up of 1 percent innovation and 99 percent imitation," said an executive.

Madison Avenue imitated radio and borrowed a stereotyped lineup of artificial voices, unlike any used in natural, straightforward conversation among people. The voices include the overpowering, unctuous, superior, wheedling, pseudo-jolly, intimate, the peep-show whisper, baby-talk, hokey-jokey, unschooled housewife, twangy hick, and many other aberrations. An observer said that the confidential voice, for instance, sounds like someone peddling hot hubcaps.

A few admen have tried to use pleasant voices that would address the audience naturally. Almost impossible to find among professional announcers, the natural sound could be achieved by some able actors. When innovators played their audition records for other agencymen and advertisers, the reaction was invariably negative: "But he doesn't sound like a professional announcer. Why can't we get a pro?"

Furthermore, the insistence was on using only the most-heard announcers. Those with a familiar voice and the accustomed "advertising sound" were most acceptable on Madison Avenue. The fact that such voices adhere to a pattern of sound which makes most ears tune them out automatically as "Ugh, more advertising!" makes little difference to admen. Their safest way to acceptance among their cohorts is to repeat the familiar—the *un*natural.

The same is true of the types of people used in TV commercials. The housewife must be either a glamor girl who has never bent over a dishwasher except in front of the TV camera, or a harsh-voiced, supposedly comical drab whom you'd shudder to have for a neighbor, and fortunately never encounter in real life. People like the boss and the mother-in-law, who are the targets of "odor" attacks, are stereotype caricatures unlike anybody you know.

Why do commercials picture such a phony never-never land? The artificial standards for radio voices spawned a similar abnormality in TV toward exaggeration. What matters if a shrieking, pop-eyed housewife in a commercial disgusts women who are potential product purchasers? What counts is that adman can nudge adman and burble, "Isn't she the most gruesome ever?"

A man from Mars could hardly find anything more ridiculous in our modes and mores than laundry product advertising, especially on TV commercials. Their inanity is compounded by the fact that the bad examples are inevitably followed by worse imitators. An advertising trade magazine reported a housewife as saying, "I have yet to see a television commercial for a household soap that wasn't an insult to a woman's intelligence." An irate gentleman damned TV's emphasis on "the dull, the mediocre, the meaningless."

A typical "people-talk" commercial for Final Touch Fabric Softener showed two young couples on a suburban terrace. The jovial white-toothed slick-haired husbands—unlike any you ever saw outside of a model agency—are about to take off for a tennis game. But there's trouble a-brewing. . . .

Wife A looks worried. Wife B asks what's bothering her. Wife A wails something like, "I feel awful that my Fred's tennis shorts aren't as white and don't hang as well as your Tom's tennis shorts." Wife B tells her all about Final Touch, which makes her Tom's tennis shorts look so whitest white and hang so well. With this cleared up, presumably they all live happily ever after.

Is that what "young marrieds" are talking about these

days? Those I asked retorted: "It's an insult to our intelligence."

Perhaps not quite so demeaning to women is the epidemic of "action" gimmicks that hit the boob tube. In an Ajax Powder Cleanser commercial, as a housewife is being shot out of her kitchen as though from a cannon, she clenches the product that "gets you out of the kitchen fast." Comedienne Selma Diamond on Johnny Carson's "Tonight" show said that the government could save a lot of money by sprinkling the cleansing powder on astronauts and "off they would go into space to the moon."

A teacher asked his class to write a composition on "What I Think About Advertising." One future housewife wrote: "If you want my opinion of advertising, well, it's there so I have to accept it, but I despise it. For instance: There's a new 'miracle' product that cleans so fast you fly out of the kitchen. My mother naturally bought it and washed the supper dishes with it. She flew out of the kitchen all right, after eleven P.M. Do you know where she flew? Right into bed to collapse." Another student wrote, "On TV most advertising is fake."

Ajax Laundry Detergent featured a white knight who was "stronger than dirt." He raced around on a white charger, touching various persons, such as a street cleaner, and turning their clothes dazzling white. One woman said she was going to hang her dirty clothes on the line and, "Let that creep on the white horse come along and turn them clean—or I'll sue the advertiser."

I would nominate as worst-of-the-worst the Fab commercial "for a wash that is wedding white . . . you look like a bride every time you use Fab." In this epic, a swarm of women of all ages walked into a laundry room and their clothes were transformed from house clothes into bridal costumes by using Fab. When this was described to a visiting European at a dinner party, he refused to believe it. The hostess told him, "I'm with you. Even watching the commercial I couldn't believe that anything so imbecilic would be thrown at people anywhere!"

"The giant in the washer" sent up out of the tumbling water, his hairy fist gripping a box of Action Chlorine Bleach. This aimed to prove that Action is "a giant of a bleach." A commuter grumbled that he hated leaving his pretty wife at home with that giant in the washer. "How do I know," he complained, "that he *stays* in the washer?"

How do such wild advertising devices come about, all in the same field of products, in a festering rash? Primarily it's a matter of one agency and advertiser trying to be more clever, dramatic, and impressive than the competitors. An adman admitted, "It's just another case of follow the leader." One launches a wacky idea and all the others panic to top it with a greater exaggeration.

Rosser Reeves, Bates agency chairman, called such gimmicks "vampire video" which "suck strength away from your main story . . . [making] commercials often dazzling in their art, but miserable as salesmen." Yet Mr. Reeves' agency created some dillies, such as scenes of fashionable ladies in white gloves eating M & M's candies without getting any messy chocolate on their pristine gauntlets.

George Wolf, vice president and TV executive at Lennen and Newell (Number 19), stated, "We're fascinated with anything that tells a story in a new and different way. The 'gimmick' commercials are interesting. Anything that makes the point is valid." Whether it makes the sale is a secondary point.

To check on the effect of the gimmicks I donned a sweatshirt, gathered some wash, and stopped at a couple of laundromats. I started a conversation with several women about the TV fantasy commercials and asked them which ad applied to which product.

After deliberation, one ventured, "Well, the white knight is Fab's—no, that's the green giant, no, I mean the giant fist. . . ."

"It is not. The ten-foot-tall washer is Dash—or is it Ajax?"

"You're wrong, it's Tide. No—Salvo—or is Salvo the bulldozer in the kitchen—or is it the lady plumber?"

Others tried to link each product with its matching TV

commercial gimmick. The result was utter confusion and bewildered laughter. Then a large lady asked, "Does it really matter? None of us pays any attention to those commercials anyhow. They go in one eye and out the other. It's like they're put together by a bunch of kids playing with their toys. The advertising people can't be stupid enough to think we believe that stuff or are impressed by it."

Another summed up, "Who's got the patience or time to pay attention to all that nonsense? And then to remember who's advertising what? And who cares?"

"Then how do you choose your brand?"

One said instantly, "I usually go for the special offer—cents off, a coupon deal, two-for-one, like that, y'know? I grab whatever seems to be the best buy in the supermarket. Of course if I find a product is terrible, I won't buy it again at any price. If I like one very much I stick with it, or maybe go for another only when there's a specially big bargain. They're all pretty much the same anyhow." The other women nodded agreement.

Hundreds of millions of dollars are spent annually on advertising and promotion of laundry products, using such idiotic approaches. You can be sure of one thing in regard to the commercials described here—they will change and be replaced by worse.

Even gorillas won't take it. In an experiment in the Bronx Zoo, four gorillas calmed down from their bickering and brawling when a TV set was placed just past the bars outside their cage. As with benumbed children, the pictures on the screen acted as a tranquilizer. However, one of the biggest gorillas started tearing up badly at times. "My theory," said Joseph A. Davis, the zoo's curator of mammals, "is that he behaved this way during commercials."

A medical journal reported on a West German study that poodles who watched TV for several hours daily suffered from loss of appetite, became snappish and very nervous; parakeets came down with fever. TV and its commercials can now be indicted for cruelty to animals as well as humans.

Each year brings new outbursts which are quickly imitated. At this writing the follow-the-leader troops of Mad-avenuers are on the trail of *tigers*. Like the other trends, it's easier to follow than to lead or innovate, especially when the client says, "Hey, that's a clever tiger campaign those people are running—I want one just like it."

Esso tells you to "PUT A TIGER IN YOUR TANK." In France it's "METTEZ UN TIGRE DANS VOTRE MOTEUR." In Germany, "PACK DEN TIGER IN DEN TANK." In a popular joke a mama tiger asks her mate, "Where have you been? You smell like gasoline."

Soon Pontiac LeMans and GTO became "QUICK WIDE-TRACK TIGERS." Another car became the Sunbeam Tiger. The modest Ghia was termed "a pussycat." There appeared U. S. Royal Tiger Paw tires, Tiger Coats, Tigertail Drink by Julius Wile, Tiger Tails bubble gum, Tigress Perfume, Tiger Sandwiches by Seeman Brothers, and Tiger Beast bracelets by Abraham and Straus.

If you "feel like a tiger is in your throat," reach for Guardets lozenges. Bovril "turns your cub into a tiger." You "make like a tiger" with Chenango Deodorant for Men, reminder of a cartoon caption in an advertising magazine: "The client says that the deodorant ad smells." A new men's cosmetics line was named "Tom Cat," with the slogan: "A Tom Cat is a Tiger State of Mind."

Ideal Toy Corporation offered a new game, Tiger Island. A hamburger stand sign advertised "PUT A TIGER IN YOUR TUMMY." Painted on the back of a lumbering truck: "I GOT A TURTLE IN MY TANK!" Tiger Beer in the Japanese *Times* sloganeered: "PUT A TIGER IN YOUR TANKARD." Standard Rochester Beer countered: "PUT A TANKARD IN YOUR TIGER." Purina Cat Food meowed: "PUT SOME TUNA IN YOUR TIGER." Goldblatt Brothers in Chicago advertised "A TIGER OF A SALE . . . SAVAGELY SLASHED PRICES." An ad for Arthur Murray Dance Studios asked: "ARE YOU READY TO R-R-ROAR? . . . BE A TIGER, STARTING RIGHT NOW!"

Why the chase for tigers on Madison Avenue? President Truman's remark probably sums it up: "Within the first few months [after being in office] I discovered that being a President is like riding a tiger. A man has to keep riding or be swallowed." The frantic adman chasing ad trends fears that he has to keep running or be swallowed by the competition.

English essayist Walter Pater suggested that happiness is "the attainment of a true philosophy." Peanuts of cartoon fame gently defined happiness as a warm puppy. Admen hopped the happiness band wagon, of course, and offered far easier solutions. Esso ads stated that "HAPPINESS IS A QUICK-STARTING CAR!" Thus, turning on happiness became as simple as turning an ignition key. Or: "HAPPINESS IS BEING ELECTED TEAM CAPTAIN—AND GETTING A BULOVA WATCH!" Brancusi furniture claimed: "HAPPINESS IS A $49 TABLE." Cone Sporterry: "HAPPINESS IS GIVING DAD A TERRY SHAVE COAT FOR CHRISTMAS." A Las Vegas hotel: "HAPPINESS IS THE SANDS." A decorator: "HAPPINESS IS A BATHROOM BY MARION WIEDER." Miss Clairol: "HAPPINESS CAN BE THE COLOR OF HER HAIR." Lest there be any mistake about degree: "REAL HAPPINESS IS BEING AT THE PUERTO RICO SHERATON."

An ad boasted: "HAPPINESS IS READING [and advertising] IN *Holiday*." This inanity is in contrast to the thoughts of a nineteen-year-old Peace Corps volunteer from Iowa in a *Holiday* article: "Happiness is the realization that one's efforts and one's work have been worthwhile." Another teen-ager wrote: "My two strongest convictions are that man can attain happiness only through selflessness, and that every man has a profound responsibility to his fellow man." Statements like these by the "juvenile delinquent generation" spotlight Madison Avenue's pursuit of the happiness theme as sick-sick-sick. A psychiatrist said, "Such callous debasement of what constitutes happiness must weaken the traditional American concepts of high ideals, especially with the very young."

Turning to liquor advertising, the same approaches are used so often that they've lost meaning for anybody, including agencies and advertisers. Agencymen alibi that liquor advertising restrictions are so strict that they prevent any creativity, although Madison Avenue boasts of a bottomless well of ideas.

Practically every liquor has been promoted for years as "light." The beers too are "light." Piel's, like others, promoted it both ways: "THE LIGHT BEER MADE FOR MEN—HAVE A BELT OF PIEL'S"—thus trying to tab it as the light beer with a wallop.

An adman explained, "We must describe a whiskey as 'light' or it's hard to get the campaign okayed by the client. Research and sales trends show that drinkers want their whiskey 'light,' not heavy. So whether the brand is actually 'light' or not, we say so. What can we lose?"

A Chivas Regal ad showed scraps of copy torn from many ads for Scotch. All claimed "lightness." Included were "world's lightest Scotch" and "first light Scotch." The headline scolded: "COME, COME, GENTLEMEN. ONE OF US HAS TO BE KIDDING." (Or lying?) Then the baffling follow-up: "What we mean by 'lightness' is smoothness"—the meaningless compounded by the trite.

I stopped after counting over two dozen ads that called each different brand "smooth," including Martini and Rossi Vermouth, which claimed to be not only "smooth" but also "serene." A Johnnie Walker Red ad asked the obvious question: "With over 208 to choose from . . . how can you select the Scotch that's smoothest?" Of course you can't. So Johnnie Walker Red says, "just smooth"—then, lest this appear too modest, adds, "very smooth." Nevertheless, the same advertiser didn't hesitate to acclaim Johnnie Walker Black as "the world's finest Scotch." With over 208 brands to choose from, how can anyone truthfully name the one Scotch that's "finest"?

"Gentleness" became a popular descriptive. Old Angus Scotch is "gentle as a lamb." House of Stuart Scotch is "gentled." Bellows Partners Choice Whiskey boasted that its "gentle taste is even gentler" and now "pours from a gentle-shaped bottle." Man, that's gentle!

As softening of the adman's brain progressed, a new campaign appeared for Calvert's Soft Whiskey—it "does anything any other whiskey can do. It just does it softer." What was "soft" to one brand was bound to become "softest" for another. Maker's Mark bragged that it's "the softest spoken of the bourbons." Michter's Whiskey "sips softly." Inver House Scotch advertised: "Soft as a kiss."

When greater safety in cars became a national issue, auto manufacturers voiced pious approval—and yet they increased the emphasis on model names suggesting wildness, ferocity, and speed: Barracuda, Wildcat, Mustang, Cutlass, Le Sabre, Rocket, Impala. Ford marketing consultant Stanley Arnold planned the image of the Cougar as "a car with some bite in it." Satirist Russell Baker then suggested specialized names, for example, to appeal to the gourmet: Dodge Soufflé, Oldsmobile Ossobucco, Pontiac Eggs Benedict; and for timid drivers, Chevrolet Chicken.

The sex-silly ads are always popular on the Madison Avenue sheep run. Revlon aimed to lure women with "COLORS ON THE NAKED SIDE." Fabergé showed a sultry striped exultantly female female: "WILD! IS THE WORD FOR THE UNINHIBITED JUNGLE BEAT OF TIGRESS PARFUM EXTRAORDINAIRE." Ondine Perfume cautioned: "SAVE IT [Ondine] FOR THE REAL MEN IN YOUR LIFE. MEN WHO WANT YOU ALL TO THEMSELVES . . . AND KEEP YOU OUT TOO LATE . . . DON'T WEAR ONDINE UNLESS YOU MEAN IT."

"THAT GLEAM IS BACK IN GEORGE'S EYE . . . AGAIN." The photo showed a leering George in bed, tousling his wife's red hair. Why the imminent attack? He switched to a Serta Perfect Sleeper mattress, offered as the modern man's aphrodisiac. Sealy mattress chipped in with the headline: "AFTER THE PILL: POSTURPEDIC."

Admen disavow blatant sex in ads, but they get as close to the borderline as possible to try to make sales. National Oil Fuel Institute devoted over three quarters of its ad to the question: "IS YOUR WIFE COLD?" Others: "KAYSER IS MARVELOUS IN BED." "WHAT MAKES A SHY GIRL GET INTIMATE?" "WHEN A CHIC WOMAN UNDRESSES, WHAT DO YOU SEE?" "TIFFANY EUBANK WON'T WITHOUT HER GREEN STRIPE [Scotch]."

Howard Clothes headlined: "HOWARD MAKES CLOTHES FOR MEN WHO MAKE LOVE." "HOWARD MAKES CLOTHES FOR MEN

WHO MAKE BABIES." Mort Wimpie of Howard's agency explained that the basic idea is to get across that Howard makes clothes for men who do all the normal things of life: "The headline is an empathy pitch—an unsubtle phrase, but it hits an empathy button." Not long after, Howard changed the theme, the advertising manager, and the agency.

Photos of sultry come-hither women highlighted ads with headlines: "PERHAPS WE COULD, PAUL. IF . . . YOU OWNED A CHRYSLER." "MOVE UP TO CHRYSLER, MARTY. WE'LL MAKE IT EASY." An agency spokesman asserted that the ads were not meant to be sexy. The adman's defense is generally, "Only a dirty mind will read something dirty in it." Every insider knows that such ads are planned specifically to appeal to the "dirty minds" which admen believe are in the majority. Otherwise they wouldn't stake millions of dollars on the ads. A lady asserted, "It takes a dirty mind to try to reach another."

In a speech, Fairfax M. Cone, chairman of the executive committee of Foote, Cone and Belding (Number 6), said: "We are now engaged in making a great deal of advertising a joke. And the question I think we must ask ourselves is whom are we kidding? When someone asks me whom I think we are talking to, whether we think the public is mentally defective after all, or what, I can only blush a deep dark red." Later he said, "The best test of any advertisement is this: could you say it to a friend without feeling like an idiot?" He's the adman who dreamed up the line: "AREN'T YOU GLAD YOU USE DIAL SOAP! DON'T YOU WISH EVERYBODY DID?" One wonders whether Mr. Cone tries that on his friends.

Words composing offensive or silly statements and empty promises are used repeatedly, mindlessly, imitatively, as admen tramp on each other's heels in the chase for your dollar. James Bryant Conant of Harvard said about the dangers of such misuse: "Some of mankind's most terrible misdeeds have been committed under the spell of certain magic words or phrases."

Chapter

TV COMMERCIALS—CROWDED, "MOST UNPLEASANT BURPS"

10

Alfred Hitchcock, master of suspense, said: "Seeing a murder on television can be good therapy. It can help work off one's antagonisms. If you haven't any antagonisms, the commercials will give you some." The commercials discussed here are not exceptionally horrible examples. They're the rule in what has been called "that great big garbage disposal plant in the sky."

A viewer fed to the eyes with TV commercials named them "most unpleasant burps." Jerry Goodis, president of Goodis, Goldberg, Soren Advertising Agency in Toronto, told the Ottawa Advertising and Sales Club: "We cannot regulate the vast amount of shoddy advertising that reaches us from below the border. . . . American advertisers and agencies . . . manage to produce the worst commercials in the world. There is nothing in the world to touch a bad U.S. commercial for triteness, for intention to deceive, and for sheer bad taste."

Pleasant, informative commercials can make solid sales sense, as proved by Margaret Buchen, a retired vice president of Kraft's agency, J. Walter Thompson. She explained that when the new medium opened up, "outside 'experts' were hired to do the commercials . . . full of sound—ringing bells, slamming doors, and the he-said-she-said kind of thing. After two weeks it was clear that the message was anything but clear. So I did what seemed sensible—wrote friendly, simple 'good eating' commercials, and suddenly Kraft products began moving fast." The same type of "how-to" commercials, concentrating on preparing food tastefully, have helped keep Kraft Foods moving fast since, year after year.

Occasionally a sponsor complains, "If only I could get across that our product is better than our commercials." Then why aren't commercials better, more informative, more bearable? There are three primary reasons: First, most all commercials are compounded of unreality seasoned heavily with bad taste and relentless high pressure. This is due to the adman's conviction that the average viewer is a nincompoop, a knucklehead, and a clod—terms I've heard applied continually in agency/advertiser meetings.

Second, most commercials are not written primarily to reach you, but *to impress other admen*. Many Madavenuers, I believe, don't consciously realize this fact themselves. Admen producing commercials look first for the gimmicks, camera tricks, "new" twists that will bring a reaction of "Oh, how clever!" from their peers and bosses. TV commercial writers and artists want to impress their personal originality on others in the creative departments, the agency, other agencies, on the client, other advertisers, the TV production field in general. Everything stems, however insensibly, from this overriding self-interest.

Innumerable times I've been accosted by advertising acquaintances in this way: "Hey, did you see my new commercial for Glimmix on TV last night?"

"Yeah . . . but I didn't get it. Seems to me it didn't sell Glimmix."

"Who the hell cares about that? How about those fast cuts, limbo shots, and split screens? And that fabulous twist with the distorting lenses, and then the tom toms and brass blasting in on the supers? Man, that's real genius stuff! It won me an award and a fat raise."

As agencymen concentrate on pandering to their personal gains, they pour in a costly cacophony of background music and sound effects to obscure the verbal message. I saw a deafened admanager rise up in the screening room in the middle of viewing the "rough cut" of a new commercial (the stage before the finished print shown on TV). He yelled above the din of brasses and strings, "Cut out the goddamned music! I ain't sellin' music and sound effects, goddamnit, I'm sellin' dog food—I HOPE!"

A weary, basically honest TV commercial specialist confessed, "With all the clever, prize-winning hogwash I've created, I often think that the best commercial would be this: Show the product in use clearly. No grinning, gibbering announcer. Say the name and the main selling point pleasantly, so everybody would hear it and get it. No tricks, clips, or zooms. At least TV viewers would know what we're selling." He shook his head. "And I'd lose my job in a week for not impressing the client with the agency's originality and brilliance."

I agreed, "When up to fifty people are milling around a stage set for a day or two of filming a minute commercial, you'd better not wind up with something clear, simple, and uncluttered."

The third major irritability factor in commercials is repetition. The reiteration of the same faces, voices, and phrases becomes meaningless as well as maddening, like a cracked record producing babble. After you watch a simpering announcer mouth the same platitudes for the *n*th time, his insipid expression seems like a monster's leer.

Repetition in print ads is effective because you can take or leave the repeated ad—without annoyance. Add sound, actors, action, and the abrasive interruption of a program's flow—and the repercussion unsells you. Admen defend themselves: "How can we avoid rerunning spots dozens of times when commercials cost tens of thousands of dollars to produce?" They must find ways to produce less irritating commercials at lower cost if that's the only course to avoid abrasive repetition which turns viewers *against* products and advertisers. Just as surely, the stupidity and unreality of commercials can be eliminated by creating for an above-moronic viewer.

As stations increasingly rule that the commercial, not the

program or audience, is of total concern, sudden cuts to commercials bring about situations like this: At a tense point in a movie, Cary Grant pushed away Ingrid Bergman and said, "I'm sorry, darling, I love you but I can't go on like this." The lovers were interrupted by a voice asking, "Darling, have you checked your deodorant lately?"

Careless placement of commercials performs a serious disservice to both audience and advertisers. During a close-up of a victim emitting a death rattle, the program cut to a forkful of chocolate cake entering a child's gaping mouth. That didn't increase the family's appetite for Pillsbury's Devils Food Cake Mix. In a play, *Portrait of a Murderer,* as Tab Hunter was entering the gas chamber, a commercial popped on for gas appliances.

An outraged viewer wrote that he sat disgusted as he watched a documentary about mass slaughter "unfold in spurts between diagrams of stomach acid and homilies on denture odors." At agency meetings I've complained, "Last night our food commercial came in the middle of a gory battle scene." The usual reaction: "What's the difference? The commercial was bright and clear—you could almost *smell* the aroma from the spaghetti and meat sauce." It didn't matter that the spaghetti reminded viewers of the entrails of wounded soldiers.

Practically every commercial is unwelcome and annoying because it interrupts the program. "One thing you can say for commercials," a viewer remarked, "you know they won't be interrupted." The late Sir Cedric Hardwicke commented cynically: "I get annoyed at the TV program interrupting the commercials. Anyone who can get worked up over a bar of soap must be a good actor."

TV commercials arouse far more animosity than print ads have ever done because you can flip past ads in a magazine or newspaper. Imagine how incensed you'd be if in the midst of reading an exciting story in a magazine you were suddenly stopped by a sealed page with big black type stating: "You can't see the rest of the story until you read these ads for Carnation Instant Nonfat Dry Milk, New Jergens Medicated Beauty Bar, Duncan Hines Fudge Marshmallow Layer Cake, and New Wesson Mayonnaise with the tasty snap of apple cider vinegar!" You'd probably rip up the magazine.

George Stevens, noted film director, went to court to try to keep NBC from "mutilating and emasculating" his picture *A Place in the Sun*. NBC proceeded with the showing which contained, according to Mr. Stevens' count, forty-two commercials and announcements. Superior Court Judge Richard L. Wells ruled against him and said, "The average television viewer is thick-skinned about commercials." Mr. Stevens countered, "I respectfully disagree with this opinion of the average television viewer, for I have heard nothing but complaints about the volume of commercials in feature motion pictures on TV."

Complaints are also frequent about the practice of spacing out commercials in the early part of a showing to "hook" the viewer, then jamming them into the second half every few minutes, spoiling the climactic scenes.

Crowding in a stack of commercials in one break is usual now; in a cartoon a viewer complained: "He said they were going to pause a moment for station identification, but instead they identified a new soap, some pancreas pills, a foreign car, and Saturday night's late movie." This blatant kind of deception, the pause for a moment, continues hour after hour, day after day. A fifteen-minute segment in a Dick Van Dyke rerun show on WCBS-TV "presented by Pillsbury, makers of light, fluffy Pillsbury biscuits," pitched commercials for Pillsbury Butter Rolls, Pillsbury Orange Danish Rolls, Playtex Cross-Your-Heart Bras, Playtex Living Girdles, Casual Hair Color, and Tame Creme Rinse, all presumably presented by Pillsbury Butter Rolls.

A priest reported that a game called TV Roulette was started for charity in his rectory. Five priests each put a nickel in the kitty daily. They turned on the set in rotation. If a commercial went on, the money went to the missions; if a commercial was not on, the priest turning the knob would win the twenty-five cents. At the end of the month, the combined priests' winnings totaled seventy-five cents—the mission gained seven dollars.

Can you expect an increase or decrease in TV commercialization? Advertisers are spending well over $2 billion on TV—plus varying estimates of from $75 million to $150 million for the production of 40,000 to 50,000 commercials annually. A checkup revealed up to thirty-three interruptions for commercials and assorted non-program messages in a single daytime hour, twenty-three interruptions in a prime-time evening hour, and six different commercial messages packed into two and a quarter minutes of a program interruption.

When the spectacularly successful "Batman" series was launched, WABC-TV took advantage of its popularity by packing in four minutes of commercials in the half hour instead of the usual three minutes in shows between 7:30 and 11 P.M. The minutes were priced at $32,000 each, over a quarter million dollars total for the twice-a-week shows, a neat gain for gluttony of $64,000 weekly. NBC crowded five minutes of commercials plus a seventy-two-second station break into each half hour of the "Tonight" show—averaging four minutes of entertainment between commercial interruptions.

When "piggybacks" (several commercials for two or more products piled into one minute) were first becoming prevalent, the Corinthian Broadcasting Corporation would not accept such commercials on their stations. Others in the industry were unconcerned, although this indifference was covered up by some fine-sounding speeches made at industry meetings against multi-product commercials.

Again, what leaders said and what they did were two different things. C. Wrede Petersmeyer, president of Corinthian, regretfully announced that they were dropping their restrictions. He stated hopelessly:

> Almost a year ago Corinthian stations adopted a policy of not accepting piggyback announcements as defined in the television code. We believed then, and we believe now, that the increased use of integrated multiple-product announcements contributes

to the appearance of over-commercialization and may retard the growth of television's advertising effectiveness to the detriment of viewers, advertisers, and broadcasters alike. Our policy of non-acceptance was based on the belief that most of the industry would maintain a similar position. However, piggybacks are being produced by advertisers in ever-increasing volume and apparently they are now being accepted by virtually all broadcasters.

That's why you're bombarded with commercials for as many as eight or more products during station breaks. So much for the desire or effectiveness of the TV industry to regulate themselves and prevent such abuses as over-commercialization.

At a high point of criticism of commercial clutter, NBC announced an increase in commercials in its prime-time movies from fourteen to sixteen. At $57,000 each, this would increase revenue close to $12 million a year—a bitter pill for the public to swallow, but delicious to the network.

Furthermore, long after NAB code director Howard H. Bell publicly expressed increasing concern over the issue of loudness in radio and television commercials, many still blast out of the set, far louder than the program itself. Similarly, complaints about crowding in a mass of short and long announcements called in Madavenese "piggybacks, promos, billboards, bumpers, and hitchhikes" have brought little effective action.

Nevertheless, when the Federal Communications Commission sought more control, Representative Walter E. Rogers of Texas introduced a bill to prohibit the FCC from regulating the amount of time a station could give to commercials. The prohibiting bill swept the House by a lopsided margin. At a luncheon meeting thereafter, during a convention of the National Association of Broadcasters, the mention of Rogers' name brought a spontaneous standing ovation.

At the same affair, broadcast news editor Jack Gould of *The New York Times* reported that E. William Henry, FCC chairman, "took to lecturing the broadcasters on the evils of short-term profits supplanting long-range wisdom. The broadcasters took the barb with complete, almost indifferent calm; they knew the bite was not there." You might ask, "Which side is *my* Congressman on—the people who elected him, or the television and advertising industries?"

An article in *Holiday* magazine reported: "A recent network drama ended at 8:24:47 P.M. It was followed by cast credits, trailers for next week's show, two sixty-second commercials, network identification, promotion blurbs for three other shows and two station-break commercials. At 8:30 came the network color insignia, a show title, a teaser opening, more show titles, acting credits, two sponsor billboards and a sixty-second commercial. At 8:35 the viewer, if still watching, had waited ten minutes and thirteen seconds for the next show."

With little effective control or restraint on the content of TV commercials, and on the loudness, frequency, and length of announcements on most stations, *Advertising Age* came through with the most naïve headline of any year: "HOUSEWIVES DON'T LIKE TV ADS MUCH."

Chapter 11

DOES ADVERTISING CONTROL TV PROGRAMMING?

"While television is supposed to be 'free,' " wrote Walter Lippmann, "it has in fact become the creature, the servant and indeed the prostitute of merchandising."

Why is it that advertising lures, embodying a sizable percentage of permissible lies, spew forth so offensively on TV? The free rein is based on the fact—usually denied publicly by admen—that advertisers control television programming to an overwhelming degree. When John Schneider was appointed president of the WCBS-TV network after the sudden dismissal of his predecessor, James T. Aubrey, Jr., he was asked in his first hasty press conference how he rated the importance of advertising to TV. He said flatly, *"It's the lifeblood."* This admission was not applauded in Madison Avenue's inner sanctums.

Such domination by advertisers is particularly significant since over 100 million people view TV programs in a single day. About 60 percent of programs and TV time pounding this tremendous audience is bought by just five advertising categories of sponsors—detergents, drugs, food, tobacco, and toiletries. These few industries, plus others such as auto manufacturers, wield staggering power: They decide what programs you are *permitted* to see.

News and public-affairs programs are influenced also. Fred W. Friendly resigned as president of CBS news because he was overruled about scheduling Senate Foreign Relations Committee Vietnam hearings. Instead the higher-ups ordered no change in programming—"a business, not a news, judgment." Friendly agreed with Ed Murrow that: "The top management of the networks, with a few notable exceptions, has been trained in advertising, research, sales or show business. . . . They also make the final and crucial decisions having to do with news and public affairs."

There is increasing evidence of interference with televised sports events in order to permit profitable placement of commercials to fit into network schedules without replacing regular commercial programs. Colleges have delayed games to later hours, inconveniencing stadium fans, to suit network and sponsor demands. Commercials have blacked out exciting play in the late innings of World Series games. Even in heavyweight world championship fights, colorful scenes of high excitement in the ring have been blotted out by grating, inane commercials.

Because I had written, produced, and represented sponsors on many radio shows, I was in on programming and advertising from the beginning of the new glassy-eye medium. From the start the question was never, "What programs will be best for the public?" The one primary deciding factor was, is, and—as things stand now—will be: *"Will an advertiser sponsor this show?"*

Advertisers pay enormous amounts hourly into the TV cash registers. A program on the NBC-TV network of about 203 stations during the highest-listening nighttime periods at this writing costs the sponsor $88,000 per half hour, with prices rising. Add to this cost about $25,000 or more for the program itself ("Dr. Kildare" was $47,000 an hour just for the program, and many others cost more). That's a total of more than $110,000 for the sponsor to run a few commercials in a single half hour of a popular series. With this huge expenditure, sponsors demand and get rigid control of programming, directly or obliquely.

Currently the advertiser specifies what program he will

buy into or next to. He doesn't buy a one-minute commercial between 7 and 10 P.M. He states that he'll buy a one-minute commercial only if it appears in "The Man from U.N.C.L.E." or "Bonanza," for example. Thus the advertisers control what programs go on the air, even though they don't create and produce the shows. Programs that sponsors won't support are canceled before they are even exposed to you. You don't have an opportunity to express your judgment of a proposed show's merit or lack of it.

The TV system is very much as though one advertiser would tell the editor of *Ladies' Home Journal* that he would only buy an ad on a page adjoining a mystery novel by Agatha Christie. The advertiser would not actually order and print the Christie novel, but he would be specifying the editorial content of the magazine through the weight of his dollars. Exit freedom of editorial judgment—as on television.

TV Guide has affirmed that advertisers specify TV programming with repeated reports such as this one about a 1964 new season's offerings: "After all these years, the networks were finally in a position to take charge. They, not the advertisers, were in the saddle. So the networks made their announcements of shows and time periods. No takers among advertisers? Out came new announcements of other shows and other time periods."

Another issue recorded the epitaph for three proposed new CBS shows: "Sponsors have been hard to find." Another item: "NBC has canceled out 'The Thirteenth Gate,' science fiction series. . . . No sponsor interest." That's the death sentence for program after program: No sponsor interest.

Sponsor control affects all programs with commercials, including sports. The facts disprove vehement denials in the sports field. One instance: Mel Allen, TV and radio announcer for the New York Yankees baseball club, was replaced by Joe Garagiola. Many surprised people wanted to know a reason.

Newspapers reported that "the sponsor and the Yankees" had decided it was time for a change. The primary sponsor was Ballantine Beer.

Neither the station nor the Yankees nor you have even the smallest voice in telling Ballantine how to make beer. On this point, Ballantine officials would undoubtedly say, "Ridiculous! What do baseball experts or fans know about making beer?"

You might ask, "What do beer makers know about running baseball telecasts?" They know how they want their commercials delivered—fair enough. So they figure they can dictate how you should hear ball games described. And they get away with it.

Dana Andrews, as president of the Screen Actors Guild, stated: "Commercial television has emerged as nothing more than an advertising medium. Its pretense of being something more has disappeared."

Do advertisers deny that they control TV programming, and that this may be unjust to the public? Ernest A. Jones, president of MacManus, John and Adams (Number 23), addressing the American women in *Radio and Television*, put it clearly and callously: "The public . . . should be reminded that there is nothing free in this world, including television and radio entertainment, and if they are asked to pay a few minutes of their time, let them pay without whining—or go to the movies, where they will find that popcorn is fifty cents per box, plus sales tax."

He went on to tell off government authorities too: Government "should be reminded that the broadcasters of this country are businessmen and make a profit with which to sustain themselves, their stockholders, and their employees, and they must do this by selling a commodity of which there is a completely inflexible supply—time."

According to this Madison Avenue viewpoint, time does not belong to the citizenry but is ceded to business and advertising through the networks and stations. They contend that the public should be humbly grateful for whatever charity is doled out to them, for the handouts over the airwaves *they're supposed to own*. Most admen I questioned agreed with this view. Some condemned Jones' talk, not for what he said but for saying it out in the open.

Some admen still deny that agencies have control over network programming. One lied in his teeth as he said over a drink, "The networks put on the shows. We just buy them or not, according to our clients' final decisions." He was told by his client, "Save that crud for addressing booster club luncheons. We live here, remember? We see the pilot shows —and what we choose to buy is what the network puts on."

This helps explain why there isn't more originality in TV programming. The advertiser buys a show in the hope that most of you will like it, keep tuning in, see his commercials, and buy his product. Therefore he customarily tries to imitate in next season's "new" show the most popular programs of last season. If he doesn't feel "familiar" with a proposed new show, he turns it down: "I can't afford to gamble with company money."

You may have wondered in many cases why a series that started with meaty dramas quickly changed into flavorless tripe. The sponsor has probably said, "No more controversy. We don't want anyone in the audience to be mad at us and not buy our products because of such antagonism." If the producer rebels, the agencyman orders, "Either boot him out or the sponsor quits." The same situation applies to many sudden cast changes if the sponsor or his wife takes a personal dislike to an actor or actress.

Critic John Crosby blamed the decline of program quality on "advertiser control of television—the insistence on being innocuous, or offending no one . . . a disastrous thing. As a consequence, television gives mild, harmless, mindless semipleasure to a majority." He also said, "The television set has ceased being an instrument of entertainment. It's become an anesthetic."

In *TV Guide's* report on a panel of six leading producers in a round-table discussion, one said, "Everybody cries out for original, provocative material, but that's lip service, because when you really start to deal with it, everybody runs for the hills."

Leonard A. Goldenson, president of American Broadcasting-Paramount Theaters, made a resounding speech to the

National Association of Broadcasters which honored him as the industry's "man of the year." He lashed out at TV's lack of creativity, said it was "stuck in a rut," indicted TV's output, and urged uplifting innovations and improvements. He didn't mention that one of the network's chief contributions to uplifting program standards was "Peyton Place." The president of the National Congress of Parents and Teachers described the show as "froth and scum."

This happens often: Mr. Sponsor says, "I'm sick of backing the same old stuff. Bring me a program that's new, different, original—nothing like it ever done before." The agencymen leave. For weeks, even months, they run themselves ragged seeking what The Man ordered. Finally they return to his office. "Here it is," the TV head says proudly, "a program that's new, different, original—nothing like it has ever been done before. It's terrific, fabulous, fantastic!"

Mr. Sponsor looks over the presentation carefully. He smiles. "That's great," he beams. "Now I want insurance—bring me the facts proving that this kind of show has worked."

Sir Harry Pilkington, a British TV expert, declared that "the seemingly democratic ideal of giving the public 'what it wants' is so much nonsense if unaccompanied by a sufficient variety of programming to enable the set owner to exercise freedom of choice."

The advertiser says that he follows the public's preference in programs as revealed by the rating services. They pinpoint, he claims, what he is seeking: the greatest number of potential customers for his products. The significant question becomes, since advertisers control programming, and ratings control advertisers, just how accurate and dependable are TV ratings?

Chapter 12

RATINGS RULE TV; WHO RULES THE RATINGS?

From the *Christian Science Monitor:* "If newspapers based their content as much on reader surveys as the television industry does on ratings, the papers of the nation would be mostly comic strips."

There's no question, even on Madison Avenue, that most advertisers buy programs primarily on the basis of their ratings by the Nielsen Television Index (NTI). Other rating services such as American Research Bureau, Abitron, Trendex, and the TV departments of large general research companies also are consulted and have some influence on program choice.

The dollar value of each rating point can be illustrated by the cost to advertisers of the original "Dr. Kildare" show. As the NTI ratings went up, the network raised the price tag of the program. The film, without charges for network facilities, increased in three seasons from $28,000 to $47,000 per show. Now prices are even higher for many hour-long programs, particularly "specials," some of which cost over half a million dollars.

Basically here's how Nielsen ratings are arrived at: A device called an audimeter is placed in the TV sets of about 1,100 (later raised to 1,170) homes in the entire U.S. This gadget records on tape what station the set is tuned to, at what time, and for how long. The tape is removed from the set about every two weeks, mailed to Nielsen headquarters in

Chicago, replaced by fresh tape which starts recording set tune-ins for the next period.

The tapes are then analyzed. Each audimeter, in *one* home, is supposed to represent the listening habits of over 50,000 homes. That's like a meat packer tasting one out of every 50,000 cans and grading the other 49,999 as exactly the same as the one—with the significant difference that the packer has strict production controls, while Nielsen lacks even positive "people controls" to certify that each of the 50,000 homes is exactly alike. The 1,100-plus Nielsen homes are, nevertheless, figured as typifying *all* TV homes in the nation.

Nielsen then translates the analyses into rating figures. Each rating point represents about 530,000 homes. Figuring about two viewers per home as an average, each rating point stands for a million persons. The top-rated program at this writing scored about 36. That means 36 percent of all homes with TV sets tuned to the show. That represents about 19 million homes tuned in and 38 million persons watching that one show. A Nielsen rating of 20 is commonly considered "good" in the advertising trade.

The instant question arises: How can about 1,200 homes be representative of all TV homes in the entire U.S.? (It has been suggested that as TV programs deteriorate, it may be discovered that the 1,200 families who watch television for Nielsen are the only people still watching it.) This imbalance of counting one tester for tens of thousands of viewers also applies to the other types of TV rating services. The diary method, by which a few families keep presumably accurate track of their TV viewing, is also subject to the criticism that a few people represent accurately the habits of millions.

One night our phone rang. A woman's voice explained that she worked for the American Research Bureau, which supplies advertising clients and agencies with ARB ratings. She said that our home had been selected in the New York area as part of a representative sample of television owners in the community. She requested that we keep track of our TV viewing for a week. They'd send us a diary, and we'd fill it out each night after the TV set was turned off. At the end of a week we'd mail it back.

As an adman I was familiar with ARB, but our home had never been "rated" by any service before. Nor had anyone we'd ever known been involved directly. I was eager to participate for the first-hand experience. However, I felt compelled to tell the woman that we were not a typical TV home. Our children were away now, there was just my wife (an artist and painting teacher) and myself, a writer who works at home. This was certainly not a typical family group.

The interviewer insisted that ARB still considered us "a vital part of the cross-section." She gave the impression of having been turned down that evening by many people who refused to be bothered. She was thrilled that I was reacting favorably and begged me to say yes. When I agreed, her relief and thanks overflowed.

Before she hung up, I asked, "Do we get paid for keeping the diary and then sending it on to you? Since ARB is well paid by advertisers for its rating service, are we compensated with a gift or anything?" She said hurriedly, "Your compensation is the knowledge that you're helping to improve TV programming." I asked, "How?"—but was talking into a disconnected phone.

When the diary arrived, it was a lot of trouble reading the detailed instructions and remembering to write down what we tuned in, what station, what time, and how many were watching—day after day. Except for my special interest in advertising, I would not have kept the diary without compensation. Why should others go to all this trouble? Lack of payment surely must encourage carelessness and fraud in filling out the diary in many homes.

I tried to be accurate but sometimes skipped a couple of days between fill-ins. Then I could only guess at the exact times and whether my wife was watching with me or not. When I mentioned this later to an ARB representative, he responded glibly, "It all averages out." That's the usual Madison Avenue line, an evasion at best. The researchers hope these inaccuracies "average out" but they don't *know*.

Finally I finished checking off the last day and mailed in Television Viewing Diary #31119-23-0011. I never received an acknowledgment or thanks from ARB for our work on the diary. And I definitely didn't see any improvement in programming. I hated to think that the viewing habits of tens of thousands of uninvolved families in our area were going to be represented by befuddled #31119-23-0011. Similarly, one screwball home in the Nielsen NTI ratings system can misrepresent the likes and dislikes of some 49,999 other families.

When a program is rated among NTI's Top Ten, the producers, the agencymen who recommended the show, and the advertisers who bought it, all love Nielsen. They swear by its accuracy and dependability. When the program drops out of the Top Ten, the same individuals howl that the rating service is a dirty cheat, inaccurate, and unbelievable. If the show rises in the ratings once more, they switch back to praising Nielsen.

Are Madavenuers surprised at these strange and inconsistent ululations by grown, supposedly intelligent and able men? Not at all. It's par for ad biz, where the hand that is shaking yours one minute may be driving a knife into your back the next. A complete, inexplicable change-up in attitude and contention is practically the norm in advertising.

When Jerry Lewis was at the top of the ratings, during his Martin and Lewis days, there were no squawks about the accuracy of rating services. When his new program, started alone years later, laid an egg statistically, he was reported as saying: "If they put the start of the Third World War on television, and it didn't get a good rating, the networks and Madison Avenue would try to have it canceled."

Variations between rating service reports run as high as 30 percent and more. During one week "McHale's Navy" was rated 15.6 by Arbitron, 23.2 by Trendex. The producers in such a situation assert that Trendex is more dependable; their competitors, trying to sell a replacement show, insist Arbitron is the better guide.

House of Representative investigations of rating services disclosed awesome errors. A Nielsen field man is reported to have said that in one city when he couldn't find a bachelor willing to have an audimeter installed, he settled for three single young ladies for his "representative sample."

A confidential memo disclosed at the investigations in 1963, written by Nielsen's chief statistical officer: "We still do not have a planned program for selecting, training and developing good men for statistical-research operations . . . we are continually embarrassed for our lack of trained talent in important areas." For such a statistical service, the advertising industry pays over a million dollars yearly. Based on questionable data, advertisers and agencies, along with the networks, decide what programs you will see.

Inside TV it's commonplace to rig the ratings by piling in the biggest stars and advertising a show heavily to the public during a Nielsen-rating week. Nielsen once announced a change—they would *not* take a rating that week as previously scheduled. Some producers repeated old shows, others rescheduled important guest star appearances: Ed Sullivan shifted a taped Brigitte Bardot interview to a later week when the ratings would be taken.

Former NBC president Sylvester (Pat) Weaver, Jr. said about ratings: "You get into these incredible problems, like twelve audimeters doubling the rating of [one program on] NBC, which shows that you are in a never-never land, and it is just one step from the entrails of a chicken." It is incredible but true that the listening habits of a dozen families can kill a program by cutting its rating drastically.

Backed by his highly profitable research complex, Mr. Nielsen, Sr. has coolly replied to outraged criticism: "Our clients are satisfied. . . . We're like baseball umpires: no one likes them, but they're essential to the game." An adman shrugged it off: "It's the big game in town. Everybody watches the scores and bets according to them. We go along or we'd be out of the ad game in no time."

Mr. Nielsen admits that ratings don't reflect the *degree* of attention or interest of the viewer. Ratings don't tell whether those at home were even in the same room with the set or had escaped to the kitchen or bathroom or answered a phone call. They don't record whether you enjoyed, hated, or snoozed through the show.

The principal criticism leveled at Madison Avenue's obeisance to TV ratings is that advertisers buy "by the numbers" and therefore program to the lowest in mass taste. On this point former chairman of the Federal Communications Commission Newton N. Minow said: "If parents, teachers and ministers conducted their responsibilities by following the ratings, children would have a steady diet of ice cream, school holidays and no Sunday school."

The New Yorker commented: "The television industry, since its inception, has devoted its vast energy and affluence almost exclusively to discovering exactly what the lowest common denominator of the American public would pay attention to for the longest possible period, and then providing that commodity in increasing abundance."

A commission appointed by President Eisenhower announced: "Thus far, television has failed to use its facilities adequately for educational and cultural purposes, and reform in its performance is urgent." The date of this "urgency" was 1960.

That brings the analysis back full circle: The chief obstacle to programming improvement is that advertisers buy primarily according to ratings. This, in turn, controls the programming supplied by the networks, who state that economically they're forced to produce shows which will rate highest in the "prime-time periods" of 7 to 11 P.M. Therefore the minority of viewers—a minority of 20 million or more people—find few shows during "prime time," when they too, like the "mass audience," prefer to watch TV.

The networks and local stations claim that they're putting on plenty of public service and "class" programs. The truth is that most of these occur on weekend morning and afternoon hours, and other "fringe time," when people are outdoors and those at home are often too busy to turn on their sets.

These less desirable periods are known on Madison Avenue as "the intellectual ghetto."

The facts add up to this inescapable conclusion: Evening programming today is critically *un*balanced. It is not weighted to please *all* the people but is overweighted to attract *most* of the people. It is programmed for advertisers who buy according to ratings, and there is grave question about the reliability of those ratings. If TV programming were balanced to please various types and tastes of listeners, there would be a different program lineup. Obviously the variety of programs would be fairer to the total population.

It's typical of Madison Avenue myopia that so few advertisers consider the *quality* of viewers rather than just numbers of people. Philip Morris finally dropped "I Love Lucy," then the top-rated program, when they found that they were paying for too many non-smokers (and therefore non-customers) in the audience.

Praising the uplifting program "The Louvre" as "a masterpiece of television," *TV Guide* complained: "We found one fault with the audience. It was too small. The overnight Arbitron rating gave 'The Fugitive' an average of 47 percent of the audience, 'The Doctors and the Nurses' 30 percent, 'The Louvre' 19."

But 19 percent here indicates an audience of up to 20 million people. The sponsor, Xerox, figured that the commercials were reaching many more potential *customers,* not just "people," among the 20 million watching "The Louvre" than they would have among the possibly 50 million persons tuned to "The Fugitive."

Sponsors who weigh *quality* of audience are still a tiny minority. Too many admen still agree with the cynical sign produced by a station representative for agency TV departments: "I don't care if it is the Last Supper with the original cast . . . *what's the rating?*"

Chapter

RATINGS APPEAR—PROGRAMMING MADNESS ERUPTS

13

"There is something supremely reassuring about television," wrote Jack Gould in *The New York Times*, "the worst is always yet to come." One of the main reasons is the ratings race which keeps competitive madness boiling at top heat on Madison Avenue.

As soon as the ratings start appearing for the new season, new hysteria explodes among agencies, advertisers, networks, and program production companies. (Independent companies that produce programs which they then sell to the networks are known as "packagers" in Madavenese.) The new star in one season's opening ratings was "Bewitched." It took second place with a whopping 29.4 Nielsen score. What happened then to bedeviled agencymen?

Whenever new ratings appear—and that's about every two weeks—the sponsor whose show isn't even in the Top Twenty starts exhorting his agency. He demands a series "like 'Bewitched' " (or whatever the winner may be). The agency applies heavy pressure on the network, which then bellows at packagers to put together a show "like 'Bewitched.' " Many pilot films (samples for a proposed series) of programs "just like 'Bewitched' " go into production. This involves the expenditure of hundreds of thousands of dollars on pilot films which will eventually be tossed into trash cans. "It's an exercise in idiocy," said E. Jack Neuman of "Mr. Novak" fame.

But perhaps you get sick of "Bewitched" after a while. Or

you still like "Bewitched" but despise programs that are just like "Bewitched" in format but are actually second- and third-rate imitations. You're nonetheless harassed by an epidemic of dull shows haunted by witchlike characters just because the ratings reported that you liked one of them. An observer capsuled this with the comment that TV is "preeminent in followership, not leadership."

A rating service executive denied responsibility for TV ills: "We're in the position of a reporter gathering and stating the news, that is, the ratings. Yet we're blamed for the kind of news we report. It's like blaming a garbage collector for gathering garbage that smells bad. Do you think people show poor taste in watching what are the most popular programs according to our ratings? Well, don't blame us—blame the TV audience."

He continued, "Are you going to change people's viewing habits by eliminating the rating services which only add up how many sets are tuned to what program? Those who criticize the ratings are refusing to face the real problem. They should apply their efforts to changing the programming structure instead of excoriating the mathematicians!"

He was asked: "But suppose your rating methods are seriously faulty and therefore the rating figures are less than trustworthy? Doesn't that fix some responsibility for the present shabby programming structure on you?"

He started, coughed, shifted his eyes to his wristwatch. "Excuse me," he said. "I'm late for an appointment."

The recurrent question of why TV programming isn't better has many answers. One major reason is certainly that networks and stations controlled by advertisers who are only interested in the number of viewers naturally cater to the lowest mass of taste.

Arthur Miller, author of *Death of a Salesman*, commented: "It's a cliché among TV producers and advertising guys to deplore the low taste of the audience. They piously assure you they'd love to put on better stuff, but there's no market for it. Nuts. What's on TV represents the tastes of the executives, not the audience. Nobody can keep doing something involving so much time and effort unless it reflects his interests."

Said playwright Rod Serling: "If I, as a writer or producer, were to be permitted a carte blanche attitude toward my work, in which the only criterion established was that I could grab attention, I would write shows that involved incest, fornication, nudism, infidelity and perversion. I make this guarantee that I can write and produce a program called 'The Dirty Show' and I'll deliver to you 90 percent of the audience."

In addition to deliberately producing programs of low taste, the reason why programming is so poor is the tremendous number of hours that must be filled. All the plays, operettas, and other theatrical entertainments on Broadway and off-Broadway would be used up in just two weeks of TV programming during the evening hours of 7 to 11 P.M. only —on just one network. These offerings have taken months, often years of writing, preparation, production, and rehearsing to develop. Yet TV must fill these four prime-time hours, and most of the other hours, for 365 days and nights each year—not just on one network but on three, plus independent stations—and for as many as seven or more channels in New York City.

The appetite of TV is not only omnivorous but is also constantly changing. It is soon satisfied and demands new enticements. Of all the shows in the top forty a few years ago, some thirty have dropped into oblivion; only about ten are still struggling to stay. Perhaps there is not enough talent and money in the TV world to fill all the hours with programs of even mediocre quality. Furthermore, the best pay goes to creative people, week in and week out, for producing "programs of poor taste"—so that becomes their creative goal.

A mediocre program is way above TV's average standard. On its twenty-fifth anniversary of honoring excellence in TV shows, the George Foster Peabody Awards found for the previous year a "dreary sameness and steady conformity . . . the intelligent, adult television audience has been constantly short-changed." They were hard put to give any awards at all, since they found only three "bright spots" in *the entire year's programming.*

A 1967 Roper Poll, paid for by the Television Information Office which is supported by the TV industry, revealed that the public feels more than ever that TV is a "vast wasteland" (as labeled in 1961) and that "broadcasting has failed to meet its obligations." Recently TV has been labeled "Cluttervision."

Still the closed minds of most admen and most TV producers form a blockade against improvement, innovation, and new talent—in spite of their protestations to the contrary. An aspiring writer who had sold in other fields said, "It's harder to break into TV than into Fort Knox." There's no point in a new writer sending a script to a TV producer; it won't be taken from the envelope unless offered by an "in" agent. And TV agents won't read material from unknowns.

Typically, a successful professional writer read that critics and viewers were starting to complain of the deteriorating quality of "The Defenders." He sent the producers a one-page outline embodying a unique legal situation which he'd never seen dramatized on TV; he asked for the opportunity to discuss and write this as a play. He received the brush-off: "We are not interested in obtaining any unsolicited material at the present time, as we are fully committed for the current season." It is significant that this turned out to be the last network season for the sinking series.

The same producers constantly bewail the lack of creative writers for TV. With rare exceptions, producers want new talent "with an established reputation."

Those in charge keep playing it safe by using the trite outpouring of "name" writers whose deadly production-line scripts have brought all the negative criticism in the first place. Such "in" writers usually blame the producers, networks, and sponsors for the inferiority of much TV drama. One of the more fearless "names," Ron Alexander, said that he would rather starve in the theater than grow fat on TV: "Too often TV operates out of fear and the safe course. . . .

The writer has no control. Sometimes you look at a television show with your name on it and wonder who wrote it." Fred Allen put it this way: "I'd rather work in a *friendly* psychiatric ward."

Novelist Merle Miller and his collaborator Evan Rhodes filled a book with their troubles in trying to write a pilot film for a serial TV drama for CBS. The classic line occurred when Miller was told, "What CBS wants is a kind of *friendly* lynch mob scene." When this was repeated as a joke to an advertising executive, he frowned thoughtfully and said, "Why not?"

The executive went on, "Those crummy writers who think they're 'artists' give me a pain. They grab the high salary and then want to write hi-falutin' literature. They know damned well that they're expected to turn out a sixty-minute background for commercials."

One of the world's leading mystery writers was invited by a network to advise them on a new mystery series. Though wounded before, and warned not to re-enter the TV jungle, he couldn't resist the tremendous fee. A week later, pale and unnerved, he told how he'd sat at a network meeting and listened to the pilot script written by others. The consensus was that the show wasn't "right." He was asked to diagnose what was wrong and bring his comments to a follow-up meeting in a few days. He went home and diagnosed, analyzed, and filled page after page with detailed notes and specific suggestions, working late into the night.

At the next meeting he proudly handed a pile of pages to the chairman, who asked, "What's this?"

The author explained, "The suggestions you asked for to improve the series."

The chairman pushed the sheets back at him, and most of them cascaded to the floor. He snapped, "Forget it! We're off on an entirely different tack."

The gifted writer sat through the chaotic, incomprehensible session. Then he quietly collected his check, tore up his recommendations, and returned to his orderly world of writing mayhem and mysteries.

Noted TV writer David Karp doesn't blame the TV hierarchy. He stated: "The unconquerable enemy of the TV writer is not the director, the producer, or the actor, or the television network president. It is the old enemy, the tastelessness of most of the people who watch television." He did not mention that in most areas, at prime viewing hours, the people who watch television have no choice except to watch tasteless shows or not watch at all.

An intelligent viewer said: "People are fairly content to eat poor, tasteless food until they're given plenty of fine, delicious servings. That's when they realize how badly they were fed before. Same with TV. But an occasional gourmet tidbit won't do it. There must be a sufficient quantity and choice of better servings on the TV menu to satisfy and upgrade the general audience appetite."

In the opinion of veteran TV writer Sam Newman, addressing the Mystery Writers of America, the trouble is that television is "creativity by committee." He compared the TV writer to an artist trying to paint a fine picture with two other people holding onto the brush at the same time.

Another stumbling block is the confirmed belief by TV heads in creativity by conference. A few intelligent writers have tried, without success, to convince TV executives: "You can't *talk* a good program. It must be *written*, not thrashed out by assorted mentalities in a smoke-filled room. Hemingway, Faulkner, you name the great author, never wrote a masterpiece in a conference." Fred Allen defined the problem: "A conference is a gathering of important people who singly can do nothing, but together can decide that nothing can be done." Comedian Allan Sherman said about the TV conference system: "You wind up with what is left after everybody's fears have been subtracted."

Can programming improvement be expected in the near future? Since advertisers control programming, there is little likelihood of a change for the better—unless the public demands it. There is one sure way you can help kill programs you don't like. This came from Norman E. Cash of the Television Bureau of Advertising (TvB): "The public has in its hands the most powerful weapon of all—Channel O-F-F." There's a challenge for you, right from the telecaster's mouthpiece.

The outcries against dull, tasteless, and offensive programming haven't had any apparent effect to date. Clearly the protest must come from more people, be louder and more emphatic before the networks will listen and act to improve programming. As summed up by Herbert Brodkin, producer of some better-than-average programs: "It's become more difficult to sell a show of quality; I think TV will get a lot worse before it gets better—I'm sorry for the public."

For the fall 1967 television season, the networks promised that television had finally come of age, and that programming would achieve true excellence. The new offerings appeared and were summed up by a newspaper headline: "BALONEY SLICED VERY THIN."

Vincent Edwards, better known as the late Dr. Ben Casey, gave his opinion, shared by many TV hardheads: "There's a place to sell filet mignon and a place to sell hot dogs. Television is hot dogs." It's certain that as long as hot dogs are the only fare on TV at prime viewing hours, that's what people will eat. And that's what adults and children will continue to be fed as a primary diet through the bloodshot Big Eye.

Chapter 14

TELEVISION'S EFFECT ON CHILDREN

A report to the American Academy of Pediatrics, based on a study of thirty hospitalized children, revealed that they were afflicted by the "tired-child syndrome." The physicians found that this sickness came from *watching too much television*. The children, aged three to twelve, averaged three to six hours of TV viewing weekdays, and six to ten hours on Saturdays and Sundays. Their symptoms were chronic fatigue, headache, loss of appetite, and vomiting.

The parents of these children were advised to stop the youngsters from watching TV. Where this was done, they were well in a few weeks. Where drastically limited viewing was permitted, recovery was slower, taking up to six weeks. A few months later, most of the youngsters were sick again because they were allowed to watch TV at will.

In another survey of children of Air Force personnel, the TV viewing of 160 children of average health occupied two and a half hours daily, with six hours on Saturdays and on Sundays. The younger children were spending about a fourth of their waking hours staring at the boob tube. A pediatrician involved said: "They are living right inside that little box."

Who is at fault? The blame rests primarily on the *parents*. Some parents keep complaining, "TV is a terrible influence on my children." They haven't learned how to limit or prohibit the "terrible influence."

One parent reports: "We had no real trouble limiting our

kids to a half hour to an hour of TV viewing a day. In addition, we permitted special programs of outstanding merit which we usually watched as a family. Sure the kids protested. I told them reasonably but firmly, 'Now a word from *your* sponsor, me. You can watch up to an hour a day—or nothing. An hour is a lot more than nothing.' "

The parent winced. "One day we caught the kids watching over an hour. There was no TV for them for a week; I removed a tube to guarantee it. They learned that an hour a day of TV was better than none at all. After that, there was no trouble. Since they couldn't develop lengthy, compulsive viewing habits, the youngsters soon skipped watching the glass slab unless 'something special' was on."

A woman who complained at a PTA meeting that her children watched too much TV admitted that she'd never really tried to restrict them. She sighed, "The only peace I get is when the kids are glued to the idiot box. It may not be good for them, but it keeps them quiet."

She was asked, "Do you restrict the kind of programs they may watch?"

"No." Defeatedly, "The worse the program is for them, the quieter it seems to keep them. Otherwise they're under my feet."

Instead of letting TV raise our youngsters, *McCall's* magazine asked: "What shall we give the children? A sense of values, the inalienable place of the individual scheme of things, with all that accrues to the individual—self-reliance, courage, conviction, self-respect, and respect for others." Or shall we let TV substitute its shoddy values?

The pediatricians who surveyed and discovered the shocking TV habits of sick children blamed parents specifically. In most cases the parents set the pattern for the children by keeping the set on hour after hour for themselves. The kids reasoned that the TV habits of their parents were proper guides for themselves; the parents never taught them otherwise. A woman said proudly that her daughter praised her for allowing the child to watch TV at will: "Mom, I like you better than any other leading brand."

While most people agree that programming for children, as well as programming for adults, needs improvement urgently, there's no clear hope in sight. The one way to get better programs for children is to keep your youngsters from watching shows you think are bad. When a program is not being tuned in, frequently sponsors drop out, and the show is canceled. The station's prime concern is sponsorship, not the well-being of your kids.

I've interviewed hundreds of station representatives over the years from behind my advertising agency desk. They always talk about audience numbers, not quality of programs. I've worked with dozens of producers of children's shows, and with the personalities who appear as aunts, uncles, clowns, and whatnots. They all had one thing in common: Their overriding concern was how many sponsors they could land and how many commercials they could pack into each show. Some recognized their responsibility to try to make a program helpful and uplifting, but as a strictly secondary consideration.

Newton Minow, the FCC chairman who called TV programming a "vast wasteland," also said: "Some people say TV harms children. I'm not sure about that, but I do say TV mostly wastes them."

The surest way to keep children from being "wasted" is to unsuction them from the TV set. Some strong-minded parents have even thrown out the TV set. Others have discovered that during summer cottage vacations in remote places, where there was no TV set, the kids not only survived but became brighter than ever. They enjoyed other absorbing activities—reading, drawing, handicrafts, music, and so on. Admittedly it's a lot easier to tell a child, "Don't bother me—go bury your head in the TV set."

If you're against "wasteland programming," you *can* do something to put pressure where it counts. Write to stations and networks, specifying your complaints. Write to sponsors that you're boycotting their products. Then refuse to use their products, and get other families to do the same. Write to your government representatives, declaring your views.

Only enough protests from voters will bring effective action from elected officials.

One child wrote to TV entertainer Shari Lewis: "Your show is stupid and I always hate it every week, but I have to watch it because my sister watches it and we only have one television set. I hate to watch nothing worse than your stupid show so try to make it a better show this week. Your friend, Everett." At least this disgusted youngster spoke up and registered his personal viewpoint. Programming won't improve until millions of adult viewers do the same.

The Senate subcommittee to investigate juvenile delinquency reported that violence and crime programs on TV were "excessive" and "to an overwhelming degree, televised during time periods in which the children's audience is a large one." Significantly, they emphasized that such programming had not substantially decreased since 1954—over a decade before—and again in 1961 when the problem had been spotlighted in Congressional hearings and publicly.

The 1964 Dodd subcommittee report concluded: "The excessive amount of televised crime, violence and brutality can and does contribute to the development of attitudes in many young people that pave the way for delinquent behavior." Dr. Fredric Wertham stated: "Television has become a school of violence." There is still no sizable improvement visible.

Whether or not you think that programs of crime and violence and other undesirable shows for children are excessive on TV, one point is incontrovertible: *No child will be harmed by a TV program he doesn't watch.* That's the challenge and responsibility of parents—and parents alone. For the primary concern of broadcasters is not to create or choose children's shows for the good of the youngsters, but rather to keep sponsors and make money.

Chapter 15

THE CHALLENGE: GREEN UP THE VAST WASTELAND

A cartoon showed a terrified man awakening from a nightmare and gasping to his wife: "I dreamed I was watching TV, and there was no way to turn it off!" For many families who live inside the TV box, the most real thing in life becomes the plainly unreal world of television.

It thus becomes increasingly imperative to improve the quality of TV programming and of advertising, which in turn selects the shows you are permitted to see. An elected British official presented the challenge in his country this way: "Television will determine what kind of people we are."

Will Madison Avenue, or the public and the elected and appointed representatives, determine what kind of people we are? Up to now, the greatest *potential* uplifting force of the past decades has been diminished to the abysmal dimension of a bad-breath commercial.

The crux of the matter, rarely faced because so many billions of dollars and influential forces are involved, is this: *Who owns the TV channels?* The often obscured answer is that the networks and stations use channels *owned by the public—by you.* The public has never been paid for these channels—they are gifts by the government to private interests, gifts now worth millions each. Station licenses, given to individuals or groups at no cost, often are then sold by them for millions in profits. As one instance, Jack Paar is reported to have bought a TV station from its previous owners for about $4 million, and sold it for $5 million. The public received not a penny for the license exchanges.

Thus the public, through government, leased to various parties—at no charge—monopoly control of channels. If a tenant rented a building owned by you and he produced noxious odors and noises all day and most of the night, he would quickly be evicted by due process of law. If he conducted his business properly, you'd be pleased to have him as a tenant.

The same commonsense regulation should be applied to the occupants of TV channels: For misconduct, they should be evicted. Once this is done, other private interests will run the stations properly (and still profitably), so long as they face the "or else" of termination of the operating license.

This is a hollow threat now since, up to this writing, *no TV station has ever lost its license.* Regulations exist to keep a station from renewing its license every three years. The laws can be made meaningful only by eviction action. In this way, television can become public air, not advertisers' air. Harmful and unbalanced programming, overabundance of commercials, most of which are tasteless, insulting, and debasing, should not be permitted to foul up the public premises—any more than landlords should be allowed to let rats, lice, and pollution infest their buildings.

The clear-cut fact is that we will get just as bad television as we are willing to stand for, and just as good television as we and our elected representatives are willing to fight for.

Each year a few "better" programs are prepared and heralded by the networks' public-relations departments to cover up the fact that they comprise a pitifully small percentage of the schedules. I don't advocate changing all programming to please the adult rather than the child mind—just a reasonable percentage instead of a token handout.

Does the public reject "better" programming? The season that CBS offered Authur Miller's *Death of a Salesman,* fine plays had practically disappeared from the screen. Miller's play was a top-quality presentation in every respect, and was viewed by a huge audience (a cynic suggested that viewers tuned in thinking it was a murder mystery).

Thereafter, some network bigwigs virtuously announced some fine plays for the following year. Did they change their minds in the interest of better programming? Or did they decide to offer some adult plays because *Death of a Salesman* scored a dominant, totally unexpected Nielsen rating?

The TV decision-makers would never have known that such presentations could attract huge audiences were it not for the reactions to Miller's superb play. Yet they still excuse the enormous preponderance of junk programs on the basis that most viewers prefer them to high-quality presentations.

"Special" programs—single rather than series shows, filling as many as four consecutive hours—became the network rage after the movie *The Bridge on the River Kwai* attracted over 72 million viewers according to the Nielsen rating. Thus, entrenched network programming habits were changed, as often occurs, by chance rather than by fresh, creative planning.

Again, it is primarily your hand on the knob that determines what shall be scheduled, whether a series shall continue or be eliminated—granted that you're permitted to vote "on" or "off" by having a choice of better programming to vote on. Nothing prevents you from joining others in your community in a concerted viewers' strike—going on a shutoff instead of a sit-in.

Critic Louis Kronenberger stated: "Since television is Big Business operating with the help of Bigger Business, the two constitute a form of Biggest Business." This can be an enormous force for good if you force it, or for increasing debasement if you're permissive. If you elect to sit and glare at the buzzing sheet of glass, griping all the while, blame yourself for the state of your inflamed eyes and temper. *The New Yorker* showed a cartoon in which the little woman told her frowning, squinting spouse: "Come to bed, dear. You've despised it enough for one day."

If you tune out unwanted programs, alone or in concerted action with others, and so advise stations and sponsors, a change will come about. Enough people became fed up with radio so that smart entrepreneurs started FM stations featuring classical music mostly. Some alert advertisers, especially of higher-priced goods and services, found that their sales were boosted with smaller audiences. The mature listeners bought more than the masses of teens with empty pockets who were reached through rock-and-roll stations. The AM stations began to lose out. Many of them switched to programming appealing more to adults.

The U.S. public today includes over 10 million college graduates and over half of all high-school-educated individuals in the world. A few days before "The National Drivers' Test" was broadcast on CBS, a top adman commented, "It'll flop with a big, fat nothing in the ratings. People want maudlin junk, not information and challenge." Over 25 million people watched the program, over three times the size of the audiences for "entertainment programs" on NBC and ABC.

Another case: In one week I was interviewed about a new book on two popular TV network shows with tens of millions of viewers, and on the Duncan MacDonald program on WOXR "better music" radio station. The two network programs produced fewer than ten letters. The WOXR interview brought dozens of letters and calls to Miss MacDonald asking the payoff question: "Where can I buy the book?" John Nebel's all-night talk show on one radio station also sold more books than the two network programs combined.

The desires of a sizable intelligent minority cannot be suppressed forever. Networks and advertisers are realizing this, but not fast enough. At the least, the enormous pot of gold at the base of the TV rainbow must be divided up. With the cost and profit changes brought about by the revolutionary money-saving satellite TV plan, the Ford Foundation—spurred by president McGeorge Bundy and Fred W. Friendly, former CBS news head—suggested that commercial TV be required to contribute large, sufficient sums to sustain nationwide noncommercial and educational broadcasting—not the small, inadequate handouts of the past.

The possibilities for establishing adequately financed and meaningful nationwide noncommercial television are promising. I urge that the planning be primarily in terms not of "educational television," the name most used in the past, but instead as *noncommercial* or *public* television. Such programming must be informational and entertaining as well as "educational," aiming for excellence in every area.

Regardless of what strides are made in noncommercial television, efforts should be increased rather than lessened toward improvement of commercial TV programming and quality of commercials, including amount of time allotted to commercials. There is a general misconception that those who seek improvement ask that *total* programming please the "cultured" rather than the "masses." This is not true. The goal sought is that prime-time programming be set up on a fair percentage basis to please and elevate all major segments of the public.

The issue is whether commercial carriers should be permitted to continue to monopolize local and national communication airwaves which are unquestionably the property of the whole public. This the broadcasters have always done for their own profit, without providing adequate service for the entire society.

Radio, like TV, is governed primarily by the profit motive, with only token regard for public service. The radio airwaves are overcrowded with commercials, and the situation is getting worse. The National Association of Broadcasters Code recommends that stations limit commercials to a maximum of nineteen minutes out of every sixty. That gives listeners only two noncommercial minutes to every commercial minute—still a lopsided ratio.

That shocking imbalance occurs only where stations *obey* the recommended NAB code. Actually, when the FCC monitored a number of stations, they found that *there was more time given to commercials and promotional announcements than to entertainment, news, and information.* No wonder an ABC radio study revealed that three out of ten commercials "might be doing more harm than good."

A few advertisers have protested such overcrowding of commercials, only because they realize that a message jammed in among others can't do a good selling job. If advertisers canceled their clients' announcements, overcrowding of commercials would stop. But most agencies want to collect their 15 percent commission and not go through the time-consuming work of checking, complaining, and canceling commercials.

The bigger the agency and advertiser, the less time they're likely to take for checking up on radio stations and TV. Media heads often don't even know whether the commercials they order and pay for are actually broadcast by the stations. The only proof they get is a series of notations on a log sheet. A newspaper sends a printed tear sheet as evidence that the ad has run; radio and TV stations cannot send a chunk of air, just scribbles that prove nothing.

The bills are received, the advertisers pay, the agencies merrily collect their commission, charging the advertiser $1,000 and paying the station $850, according to the traditional system. The agencies believe the spots have been broadcast in spite of possible station inefficiencies, mistakes, and foul-ups—but they don't *know*. It's another dead end in the Madison Avenue maze.

Theoretically a station that offers mostly commercials and does not provide enough "community service" can't get a license renewal. But the FCC hasn't the budget or staff to check each station's programming carefully. Practically all licenses are renewed automatically, although the worst offending stations haven't even made a token attempt at "a bona fide effort to serve."

About programming in the public service, comedian Godfrey Cambridge noted: "A guy comes on the screen at four in the morning and says, 'We recognize our responsibilities as broadcasters and we now bring you an editorial.' Some say that 4 A.M. is not prime time, but that's a matter of definition. . . ."

With its practically total commitment to commercialism, no wonder—as veteran commentator Raymond Swing has stated—radio has "lost its authority . . . its stature . . . a sense of its peculiar capabilities . . . is now a haphazard, scatterbrained, and demoted participant in our national life.

. . . The exigencies of earning profits have proved to be too demanding. So now we lag far behind many countries that are poorer in other ways than we are."

There can always be a first time for the FCC to revoke a station's license, particularly on TV. It is notable that something effective occurred when New York Deputy Mayor Robert Price threatened to oppose the renewal of WNBC-TV's license. He protested to the FCC about the handling of spot commercials for Mayor Lindsay's campaign. Channel 4 grosses about $35 million annually—not a small amount to be in license jeopardy. NBC lawyers met quickly with Mr. Price and he dropped his opposition. Similar threats by citizens' organizations, and the follow-through if required, would win programming improvements.

The power of the individual can be most effectual. Whether or not you buy the product controls advertisers' expenditures and decisions. Like many other people, you may have a vital misconception about how advertisers set their appropriations. You may think that when sales drop, advertisers spend more in order to lift the sales curve. Wrong. Except in rare instances, advertising budgets are based on a percentage of sales. When sales go down, advertisers cut ad outlay fast.

If you want to get rid of undesirable programs and annoying commercials, *don't buy the sponsored products.* There are plenty of other brands, and good unbranded products, that you can purchase instead.

Your voice is the determining factor for pay TV also. This development is opposed vigorously by broadcasters, advertisers, and agencies which fear any change in their very profitable status quo. But if enough of you make your desires known, if you want pay-as-you-see TV without commercials, it will be made available eventually. This is not likely until two things happen:

1. Enough people must complain and tune out commercial TV as it now exists. Such increasing negative action will force a move by networks, stations, and advertisers to improve programming or else open the door to pay TV.

2. Pay TV must offer exceptionally appealing programs. This is a chicken-and-egg dilemma of "which comes first?". Most entrepreneurs can't afford to put on costly programs such as first-run movies if the audience isn't big enough to pay them. Yet without superior programs, people won't subscribe.

The president of the Screen Actors Guild said: "The great hope of pay TV would be that it would be an entertainment medium, not an advertising medium." This leads to the showdown question: Do enough people detest TV commercials and much of current programming to pay for what you and your family would watch on pay TV? To date there is no solid evidence that this is so.

As for *color TV,* it adds an improved dimension in telecasting effect, but the problems of better programming remain the same.

With most programs chosen according to ratings, television is directed to the youngest mentality, not to the adult mind. A responsible survey of a new season's programs found that the groups most enthusiastic about the shows were boys and girls aged six to seventeen. Least enthusiastic were women over eighteen and men over fifty. Robert Shayon in the *Saturday Review* dubbed television "a lollipop-trap."

A key consideration is this: Is it your conviction that television should be the property of the people of the U.S.—or that of advertisers? We pride ourselves on being at least theoretically in our democracy "free as air." But we have little freedom of choice as to what is programmed on the air.

This is the point where admen and businessmen start to scream about government interference, fascist policies, communist control, lack of freedom of the press, and all that easy-say, easy-fling malarkey. Nonsense! Regulation of TV cannot be compared to the press. There can be thousands or hundreds of thousands of different publications—daily, weekly, monthly, annually, or whatever the publisher wills and the public will accept. *Look* magazine stated that there are 8,758 magazines in America. But the availability of TV channels (and radio station licenses) is limited. This squeezes down to a comparatively small number of stations and only three TV networks, making available to the public, in effect, only three "national magazines" of the air.

I suggest for decisive consideration a relatively simple solution to check Madison Avenue's domination of TV programming. This is not a new or original proposal. It has been advocated by people in government and public life. It is approved by only a few admen and businessmen outspokenly, but by many more privately, although opposed probably by the majority. The solution is not government operation of stations or networks, but a transition to what is generally called the "magazine concept" of TV programming.

A general magazine publishes material to appeal to most all segments of the reading public. The advertiser pays certain fixed rates for a page ad in the magazine. Outside of paying a premium for a few select positions, such as inside and back covers, and excepting quantity discounts, all advertisers pay the same for a page.

The magazine, like a newspaper, determines where the ad will be positioned and what the surrounding editorial content will be. The same would be true for the networks and stations under the "magazine concept" for TV. The advertiser's commercial would be placed not in selected programs but in morning, afternoon, prime evening, and late evening periods with varying rates, or some similar equitable breakdown of overall time periods would be set up. The advertiser could not specify, as he does now, the program in which his commercial appears.

Thus, the networks and stations could readily provide well-rounded programming. If TV management then failed in this responsibility, the way would be clear for government to shift licenses to more able, public-spirited, and informed groups or individuals for operation within our free-enterprise, free-profit system.

Similar checks and balances would also eliminate overcrowding of commercials with its attendant abrasions and evils. From my experience, I believe strongly that most agencymen would secretly prefer this system. It would remove pressures from them to buy the top-rated show—because they'd have no voice in the program structure. Opposition is based now not on thoughtful consideration and rejection, but on blind opposition to *any* basic change.

The stations and networks must have the courage to take this inevitable step. Working out a fair and profitable rate would present few problems. I'm sure that soon the stations and networks would be making as much or perhaps more profit.

If the government-licensed stations and networks do not make this needed move to magazine programming in the interest of the *whole* viewing public, then government would have to force the change. Pressure by the public and their elected representatives for such action, first on a volunteer basis, and then by enforcement if necessary, should start *now*. The results would be best for all concerned—for business, advertising, and television interests, as well as for the true owners of the channels, the viewing public.

David J. Curtin, vice president of corporate communications for Xerox, one of the few companies supporting better programming, urged the increase of "programs that stimulate, rather than stultify, enliven rather than enervate, and challenge rather than mortify."

Television "should address itself to the ideal of excellence, not the idea of acceptability," wrote essayist E. B. White. It "should arouse our dreams, satisfy our hunger for beauty, take us on journeys, enable us to participate in events, present great drama and music, explore the sea and the sky and the woods and the hills. . . . It should restate and clarify the social dilemma and the political pickle. Once in a while it does, and you get a quick glimpse of its potential"—a potential now usually vitiated by the clutter of offensive commercials.

Right now, to an overwhelming degree, what the networks

and stations promise—and what they deliver—are entirely different things. The unenforceable Television Code of the National Association of Broadcasters states: "It is in the interest of television as a vital medium to encourage and promote the broadcast of programs presenting genuine artistic or literary material, valid moral and social issues, significant, controversial and challenging concepts." How can the promises in this commendable statement be fulfilled?

If you want TV improvement, your outcry must grow louder across the land. It must swell from the current comparative whisper into a roar sure to be heard and honored, to amplify Minow's challenge: *"As a people we must insist on television's fulfillment and we must reject its debasement."*

Chapter

CIGARETTE ADVERTISING: A SPECIAL DILEMMA

16

Next to television reform, probably the hottest single subject of controversy involving the ad world in recent years is cigarette advertising and regulation. A checkup showed that in one typical week, cigarette advertisers spend about $3 million to telecast almost 3,000 commercials urging the smoking of thirty-eight different brands; this total included single-station commercials in only the top seventy-five markets out of television's 274.

Accused of scheduling too many programs of violence, programming heads resolved the problem by keeping the same shows, or creating similar ones, but dubbing them "action programs" instead; has Madison Avenue's handling of the cigarette controversy been a similar case of word juggling? *The New Yorker* spotlighted the artifice in much cigarette advertising by discussing this sample from the comparatively early days of the smoking/cancer dilemma:

> "No Medical Evidence
> or Scientific Endorsement
> Has Proved Any Other Cigarette
> to Be Superior to KENT."

The magazine commented that "what the Lorillard people are really proclaiming, in such bold type, is that no medical evidence or scientific endorsement has proved any other cigarette to be less harmful to health than Kent."

In the face of criticism, changes were made and a new

campaign expounded: "YOU'LL FEEL BETTER ABOUT SMOKING WITH THE TASTE OF KENT." This implied strongly that "You'll feel better with Kent." Since this came dangerously close to a direct health promise, forbidden by government regulations, the Kent theme was again changed to: "LIGHT UP A KENT AND YOU'VE GOT A GOOD THING GOING." Similarly Winston switched to: "CHANGE TO WINSTON AND YOU CHANGE FOR GOOD!" The oft-repeated "good for you" inference was hardly subtle, but it was defensible according to advertisers' standards.

Cigarette advertising boasts continue to range from the phony to the ridiculous. Another Winston claim: "The best flavor in cigarette smoking." Kent "satisfies best." How could both be "best" since Salems offer "the smoothest flavor in cigarettes today"? That's contradicted in turn by Newport, which "smokes fresher—and tastes better than any other menthol cigarette."

Lark offered "a richer-tasting [than what?] cigarette—a rich flavor that no other cigarette can imitate." Other cigarettes can and have imitated Lark's use of charcoal. Similarly, Lark imitated charcoal cigarettes such as Tareyton.

Pall Mall ("and they are mild!") and Chesterfield King ("smokes so mild") stress mildness, which infers less strength. These are two of the brands consistently rated among the highest in nicotine content by independently published laboratory comparisons in the *Reader's Digest* and elsewhere.

York cigarettes claimed to be "supurb, noble, majestic, rich, sumptuous" and to have (here we go again) "the world's finest tobaccos" and "the noblest taste of them all." A smoker asked, "You used to be in advertising, so tell me—what the hell is a *noble* taste in cigarettes?"

"Nobody at the agency or advertiser's needs to know or care," I explained. "All that counts is that somebody up there who pays the bills likes and buys the 'noble' sound of the meaningless phrase." Webster defines noble as "having high moral qualities or ideals."

A group of young Canadian admen formed the More or

Less Honest Manufacturing Company, marketing a brand of cigarettes named Less. The advertising suggested: "IF YOU CAN'T QUIT—SMOKE LESS!" "IT'S WORTH MORE TO GET LESS." "LESS! SLIGHTLY MORE THAN MOST." They stated that people who couldn't cut down on smoking could still smoke Less. It made no less sense than most cigarette advertising.

E. William Henry, chairman of the Federal Communications Commission, addressing 6,000 TV and radio delegates at the National Association of Broadcasters forty-fourth annual convention, said about cigarette advertising:

> No one would ever know that a major public controversy is in progress as to the harmful effects of cigarette smoking on the American public. One would never guess that the great bulk of medical opinion, including a Surgeon General's report, has concluded there is an adverse causal relationship between cigarette smoking and health.
>
> Television viewers, in particular, are led to believe that cigarette smoking is the key to fun and games with the opposite sex, good times at home and abroad, social success and virility.

The same day's newspaper stated: "If all Americans were non-smokers, there would be 12 million fewer cases of chronic illness reported in this country, a new national survey indicates."

Cigarette manufacturers fostered the impression that just by adding a filter they were producing a safer smoke. Their prime concern was not to add the *most effective* filter to reduce impurities in the smoke. Dr. George E. Moore, director of Roswell Park Memorial Institute, New York State's cancer center in Buffalo, found in a study that Pall Mall filters, for one, produced 43.3 milligrams of tar and 2.13 of nicotine—against 32.7 and 1.75 for Pall Mall regulars.

Chesterfield filters produced more tar and nicotine than Chesterfield regulars. Pall Mall filters produced almost *three times as much* tar and nicotine as the lowest brand in the study (True filters, which produced 16.9 and 0.79 milligrams, respectively). It would seem reasonable to require by law that nicotine and tar content be printed on each pack, just as net weight is printed on food packages. This would inform the purchaser; it's the purchaser's personal option to reject or ignore the facts.

Typical of Madison Avenue's use of partial truth were the full-page newspaper ads for True cigarettes which followed the news stories two days later. These ads did *not* reveal that only twelve brands out of over three dozen cigarette brands were in the test. Naturally the True ads didn't mention either that while some filters are considerably more effective than others, none really protects against lung cancer, cardiovascular diseases, emphysema, and other deadly ills more prevalent among smokers than nonsmokers.

With the pressure of the cancer scare, cigarette companies, fearful of government interference, got together hastily and organized the Cigarette Advertising Code. They succeeded in their initial purpose: They slowed up regulatory action by Congress and the FTC. The expenditure of some $250 million a year on cigarette advertising and $3.2 billion in tobacco taxes by federal, state, and local governments adds up to a lot of political pressure.

At this writing the code is being referred to as the Phantom Code. One of its main avowed aims was to stop cigarette companies immediately from showing young people smoking, in order to have less effect, presumably, on starting youngsters smoking. Four months after the code was formulated, Viceroy ads featured young tennis players lighting up after a hot game. Salem showed a young couple playing giggly games alongside a waterfall. Newport displayed a fetching blonde nymph puffing away beside dashing waves.

A TV commercial producer admitted that it didn't matter how young the models *looked,* or how youthful were their actions, as long as they possessed "over twenty-five" birth certificates. In fact, his quest now was for older models who "looked young."

Some of the "monumental" changes insisted on by the code: Tareyton had to change the description of "white outer filter" to "white outer tip" and "an inner filter of activated charcoal" to "an inner section of charcoal." Parliament was not permitted to mention "recessed filter"—instead it could offer "a filter that's recessed in." Changes required of other brands were equally bland.

If anything ever kills cigarette smoking, it won't be the cancer scare but a reaction by smokers against the mass of cloying, debasing cigarette advertising. Ogden Nash put it this way:

> "To me the question of smoking or not smoking is
> not even slightly controversial;
> The only factor that might persuade me to
> renounce the habit is the repetitious
> theme of the TV commercial."

Regarding the cancer controversy, a leading spokesman, agencyman Draper Daniels, complained that the advertising field was again the favorite target. He said that the spotlight ignores "the tobacco growers and their powerful lobbies in both houses of Congress, and, for the most part, the tobacco industry itself."

He sighed, "So here we are today, 'The Ugly Americans' finally identified—manipulators of men's minds, immoral, martini-drinking public liars, merchants of lung cancer." He suggested, "If cigarette smoking is indeed a cause of lung cancer, then the advertising of cigarettes should be forbidden by law. Until that time it seems to me that the question of whether to handle cigarette advertising or not to handle it should be up to the conscience of each individual advertising man."

Similarly, Art Tatham, board chairman of Tatham-Laird-Kudner (Number 31), stated: "The head of a well-known agency reacted to the [Surgeon General's] report by announcing that his agency would not handle cigarette advertising. . . . His agency, however, has done some very enticing advertising for a well-known brand of liquor. Nearly every good thing can be made an evil through abuse. It's a safe bet that more people die annually from overeating than from the effects of either cigarettes or liquor."

He concluded: "Any product which may legally be manufactured and sold should not be deprived of the services of an advertising agency. . . . The choice to smoke or not is properly the choice of each individual."

Philadelphia agencyman Ron Bloomberg did not agree: ". . . the real responsibility still lies mouldering in the laps of the agencies who, after all, *create* the advertising. . . ." He suggested that all admen refuse to produce advertising "which makes smoking seem a glamorous, sophisticated, 'in,' refreshing and [incredible!] funny diversion . . . now, right now, let those of us who are not afraid of the truth make a beginning. . . ."

Most doctors I checked said that while the cancer menace of smoking is clear, other factors are not. They advise some patients to quit smoking entirely, others to cut down to a pack or less a day. One noted physician emphasized: "A few of my patients would soon have nervous breakdowns if deprived of the comfort they get from cigarettes. Others would put on excess weight rapidly with far greater danger to their health from overweight than from smoking. Each case is different and must be treated accordingly." He lit up.

Self-regulation in the cigarette industry is primarily a matter of gaining time for advertisers. Using only models who are twenty-five years old or over makes very little difference in whether youngsters start smoking or not. After the code went into effect, cigarette advertisers were not supposed to advertise on TV programs having a large proportion of "under twenty-one" viewers. A checklist of shows sponsored by cigarette advertisers included "Daniel Boone," "The Red Skelton Show," "Beverly Hillbillies," "The Man from U.N.C.L.E.," "The Jackie Gleason Show," "Wild Wild West," and many other programs with large youth audiences.

The National PTA asked for a ban on all cigarette advertising on TV before 9 P.M. This would provide a concentration of cigarette commercials on many different brands into two prime viewing hours nightly. Plenty of children and millions of teen-agers would still be watching. This barrage attack is considered a highly effective advertising technique which some advertisers use purposely instead of scattering shots all over the place.

With competition at top heat among cigarette producers, advertisers will interpret regulations to their own advantage. Rules will be badly bent if not broken, no matter what restrictions are imposed. Admen will seek out the permissible lie, the defensible subterfuge, such as "you've got a *good* thing going."

A tobacco man stated in private: "The campaigns emphasizing 'good' about cigarettes in a 'good-for-you' way are further positive proof that self-regulation is ineffectual in our cut-throat competitive business. Some advertisers will always try to get away with as much as they think possible, violating the spirit if not the letter of the code." The *Harvard Law Review* asserted: "Self-regulation cannot practically be expected to extend to self-extinction."

After Surgeon General Terry's report, cigarette sales dropped sharply, then returned to the previous level and above. The same happened in England. Will smokers change their minds and habits after further findings are presented? Advertisers are betting that an enduring downturn isn't likely, based on past performance.

Laws have been passed to force the printing of a warning message on each pack: "Caution: Cigarette Smoking May Be Hazardous to Your Health." But experience, backed by sales to date, shows that a warning on the pack will not reduce cigarette consumption. Manuel Yellen, chairman of the P. Lorillard Company, said: "I think the American public is too intelligent to pay any attention to that type of warning."

Statistics show that the health warning didn't hurt sales—in fact, sizable gains have been scored by cigarette brands particularly high in tars and nicotine, and by the extra-length 100-millimeter cigarettes which provide an extra measure of suspected irritants. The FTC suggested the slogan: "Extra health hazard at no extra cost."

Goodman Ace offered in the *Saturday Review* a correlated warning: "TV viewing may be hazardous to your health. If nausea and violent regurgitation persist, see your TV repair man."

Stating actual percentages of tar and nicotine right on

the cigarette package may lead more smokers to choose a brand with lower levels of these harmful elements, but even that is doubtful. Admen know that people may read the words on any package the first time but rarely thereafter. Ask a smoker to tell you what's printed on the pack of a brand he has smoked for years and handled thousands of times; chances are he won't know.

Nevertheless, when tar and nicotine contents are printed on the package, and included in the advertising, this at least provides a guide for smokers as to which are factually and probably the least harmful cigarettes. Hypocrisy creeps in again as the statement is added: "No health claim is intended or implied by this listing." That's obviously the whole reason for the listing, but the Alice-in-Wonderland denial is accepted by advertisers and authorities alike. Typical is Marvels advertising: "Tar and nicotine are way down," quoting from a report on thirty filter brands tested, listing Marvels content, "second lowest in tar and nicotine," and concluding: "No health claim is intended or implied by this listing" —another permissible lie presented to youngsters as an adult standard of moral integrity.

Nor could government be expected to expose smoking dangers effectively. Health, Education and Welfare Secretary John Gardner pointed out to Congress that his annual budget of a few million dollars to fight cigarette smoking was pitted against $250 million spent by tobacco advertisers just in radio and TV. When the Federal Communications Commission ruled that broadcasters carrying cigarette commercials must give a significant (not equal) amount of time to the presentation of opposite views on smoking, advertising and business rose in wrath. The National Association of Broadcasters branded the move a "dangerous intrusion into American business," and passed a resolution to fight the move in court.

Ex-TV executive Fred Friendly pointed out that station licensing is supposedly based on broadcasting "in the public interest." He wondered whether broadcasting cigarette advertising could be considered "in the public interest."

The cigarette controversy brings up pivotal questions: Should freedom of enterprise include freedom by businessmen to make and advertise a product that is a health hazard? Should freedom of the individual include the freedom to buy and use freely something bad for his health? In the American tradition, these are probably questions which each person can only decide for himself.

If you ever wondered whether advertisers are banded together to protect each other, the smoking controversy has definitely provided one "no" answer. Competitive advertisers jumped in to take every possible advantage of the situation. Cigar, pipe, and tobacco advertisers stepped up their efforts overnight, and slammed at cigarettes ruthlessly. State Mutual Life Assurance Company quickly threw in a campaign offering policies with lower rates for nonsmokers, and urged people to stop smoking cigarettes.

As for cigarette advertisers, the cut-throat theme of American Tobacco Company in introducing new Colony cigarettes "with bonus gift coupons" is typical. The theme indicted every other coupon brand as poor-tasting: "Colony . . . the first coupon cigarette that tastes as good as a non-coupon cigarette."

Dog eating dog could take lessons from adman devouring adman.

Chapter

ADVERTISING RESEARCH— OR "DAMNED LIES"?

17

"There are three kinds of lies," according to Disraeli, "lies, damned lies and statistics." Gen. Charles H. Grosvenor said, "Figures won't lie, but liars will figure." Thomas Carlyle summed it up: "You may prove anything by figures."

A modern phenomenon is the rapidly increasing encroachment on personal privacy and decision by a bombardment of facts and figures based on advertising and other research. Interviewers infringe on your time and unfettered thinking. The public is beset by questionnaires and the questionable answers and conclusions, adding up to what some psychologists call "survey sickness."

However you regard its value, you can't slough off the growth of researching in our society. "Good" research is as necessary a part of business activity today as manufacturing and selling. The question is: How much research is sound, honest, and reliable?

According to a Madison Avenue Solomon—Dutka, head of the sizable Audits and Surveys Company—businesses "are buying marketing research at an estimated $400 million a year (plus spending about $100 million in their own research departments) . . . double the amount spent ten years ago . . . twenty times the outlay twenty-five years ago." There are now over 350 independent "marketing research" concerns, many more in other branches of research related to advertising, and well over 1,000 companies with internal research departments.

The figures and conclusions of all kinds of research are important to you because they influence advertising and affect other aspects of your life. Political polls certainly have an effect on elections—minor or major, some say for good, others for evil. In all the bewildering facets of research, some fakery exists, not so much in the figures usually as in the attitudes and interpretations of some researchers.

Discussing the hocus pocus of figures, one commentator said: "Statistics are like a bikini. What they reveal is suggestive. What they conceal is vital." Pretentious absurdities abound. *The New Yorker* magazine noted: "Herewith the title of a proposed report to be compiled, at a cost of several thousand dollars, by the Young & Rubicam advertising agency for its client General Foods: 'Exploratory Interviews to Uncover Conscious and Latent Consumer Needs, Wants and Desires in the Grilled Sandwich Area.'"

Statistics can mean anything or nothing, as in the story of a timid man who was afraid to fly. A research-oriented airlines executive told him, "Calm down—the odds are a million to one that your plane will have a bomb on it." The worrier moaned, "I wish the odds were better." "That's easy," the expert assured him, "if you want better odds, carry a bomb on board yourself. The odds are at least a *billion* to one that your plane will have *two* bombs on it."

Doomsayers warn that teen-agers are an increasingly destructive force, growing in numbers. They quote the fact that Americans under twenty now comprise about 40 percent of the population. They don't mention that when the nation began back in 1776, over 50 percent of the population was under eighteen.

Pointing to great progress in his community and the nation, a politician boasted in a National Book Week speech that 220 libraries have been built in the U.S. in the past fifteen years. He did *not* mention that during the same period some 10,000 pizza parlors, 15,000 frozen-custard stands, 9,180 bowling alleys, and 3,500 drive-in theaters went up.

The misinterpretations are staggering as Madavenuers and others, most of whom have little knowledge but love to toss around figures, pompously quote research data. Their chief stock in trade is to appear *positive*, no matter how unsure they may be. A dozen different researchers can draw a dozen different conclusions from the same basic data, each insisting that only his findings are correct.

Over $6 million was spent the first year by Mobil on a probably pre-researched advertising campaign based on "megatane ratings." Three years later the theme was discarded as having failed. A company executive admitted: "The megatane experiment was difficult for the consumer to understand. . . . From a research viewpoint we received high playback on the word 'megatane,' but the understanding wasn't there." To paraphrase the comment about a fatal operation: The research was a success but the campaign died.

The statement has been made that Madison Avenue's research heads and murky psychologists would come closer to the truth if they knew a lot less—and understood a lot more. Astounding, obvious errors abound. An agency president's son, just graduated from college, took the agency's routine job-aptitude tests. The computerized report came through that the applicant was "best suited for retirement."

Frequently various types of research disrupt sizable projects and entire organizations. One case involved the advertising for a large, efficient, and very profitable corporation. Most of the directors were financiers and knew nothing of the day-to-day operations of the recently acquired company. They voted to hire a management research team to analyze the functions of executives of the rapidly growing firm.

A vice president, who was also head of sales and advertising, was a most able and creative man. He was rated high for a constant flow of fresh and practicable ideas. He resisted the consultant project. He didn't conceal his resentment of officious researchers who kept interrupting his busy hours and the company's routine as they bounced into offices with lengthy questionnaires which required immediate answers.

A major conclusion of the final report was that the vice

president was "an able administrator" but "seriously deficient in creative ability." Direct control over advertising was taken from him and shifted to another executive who had been analyzed and dubbed as "highly creative." The latter was useful as a glad-hander and "front man" but had never offered an original idea. Those who worked with him knew from experience, not from a $50,000 research analysis, that he was particularly *un*creative.

Now that research had tabbed the glamor boy as "highly creative," he believed it. He messed up the advertising so badly that sales soon began to slip. The chairman pre-emptorily shifted the advertising responsibility back to the original vice president. The directors shrugged it off, preferring not to notice the change. They'd had their expensive fun and were busy with other activities. The "$50,000 mistake" was buried in the files. The embittered executive summed it up with the worn jibe: "Instead of calling in a consultant hereafter, we'll louse it up ourselves."

A common ploy of researchers is to get across the idea fast that the common executive can't begin to understand the intricacies of their miraculous methods. Most of them speak an incomprehensible language which Madavenuers and businessmen pretend to understand lest they seem ignorant or not "in." When cornered, the researcher lowers his brows, raises his pipe, and says, as to a five-year-old, "You just wouldn't understand. . . ."

I've interrupted numberless research presentations in conference rooms to say, "I don't know what you mean by that. Please explain." The explanations were usually more garbled than the original mumbo-jumbo.

"I still don't understand."

The chairman would interrupt impatiently, "Let's get on with it. You can explain to him later."

But "later" rarely arrived. I'd ask other agencymen afterward what it all meant exactly, but they didn't know. Most preferred to remain ignorant rather than take a chance of seeming less than all-wise and losing face.

The greatest errors are made because Madison Avenue,

in its search for proof, substantiation, and alibis, honors the Great God Research too highly. Agencymen say quickly when a recommendation is questioned: "It's backed by research findings." If pressed, they scramble over to the agency research director for corroboration to show the client.

The research head, in turn, is likely to call in his staff and order: "The boss says here are the *answers* he wants. Now you dig up the facts to back him up." Armed with their freshly typed "facts," bound in impressive gold-stamped binders, the agencymen trot back to the client and pitch the presentation. It was suggested to a research director that he have lettered on his office door: "Facts Manufactured While You Wait." He wasn't amused.

Most everyone is satisfied once they're bolstered by the facts and figures. If the resultant advertising fails, all involved, agency or clientside, can alibi: "Don't blame us, we followed the research data. The fault must be in manufacturing or sales or . . . or . . . or. . . ." Whoever is blamed starts gathering research of his own to excuse his past course of action.

Research can be a great help but is rarely a cure-all as often promised. In the case of a brand of pipe tobacco, sales were dropping year after year. True to form, an agency executive insisted: "The solution is research. We'll never know exactly why sales are slipping until we get the answers through research."

Another disagreed: "Research isn't going to cure the obvious big fault. Men are now smoking milder, more aromatic tobaccos. They don't want this strong, old-fashioned bite. Advertising can't change the sales trend unless you change the tobacco blend."

"That's only an opinion," retorted the research-minded adman. He won. The research merry-go-round started whirling. One project spawned another, then another, and still another. For every statistic, a dozen more were needed to substantiate the first. Finally the costly research concluded that the biggest trouble was package size and design.

Sizes of packages were researched to select the size and

shape most pipe-smokers said they preferred. Then colors had to be researched to see whether red indicated the contents were "hot." Blue might mean "too cool." Gold might reflect "quality" but could also indicate "overpriced." Dozens of package designs were created and researched to determine the best one. Ad appeals were researched. Advertising placement possibilities—magazines, newspapers, TV, radio, billboards—were researched.

Eventually, after huge, multiplied expenditures, the new "research-proved package" was placed on tobacco counters with costly fanfare. Sales boomed as pipe-smokers grabbed the attractive new container. Sales dropped as men smoked and rejected the same old strong, heavy, non-aromatic mixture. Finally it was conceded that the tobacco itself was at fault—since there was nothing left to blame.

Walter Lippmann warned: "A good reporter should have endless curiosity plus equanimity. I mean curiosity without the desire to use facts differently from what they happen to be." On the contrary, admen often use only selected facts from broad research for a dishonest effect. An ad may state: "Product A was proved safest in comparative tests with the three leading brands." They don't tell you that Product A was proved by the same tests to be less safe than five other "leading brands."

The same research may also have revealed that the "three leading brands" were all more efficient and more economical in use. Product A was ahead *only* in being "safest"—and that to an inconclusive degree. The advertiser accents the one hazy positive, bypassing completely the significant negatives. This was pegged by a cartoon showing a tycoon telling a researcher: "Kupperman, I want your department to come up with some statistics showing we're leading in *something*."

An admanager told of a presentation made by an aggressive agency to try to land his account. Their "facts" proved that the leading competitive manufacturer in the field was getting many more sales per dollar expended for advertising. This showed up current ads as comparatively very weak, even though sales were up. Other executives of the company were greatly impressed; they were about to fire their agency and take on the new one.

The admanager interjected, "Wait. Everything in the presentation hinges on one 'fact'—our leading competitor's sales volume on their big brand. I know positively from inside information that the figure this gentleman just quoted is inflated *at least 30 percent.* That error changes all the other data and proves that our advertising is actually doing a fine job competitively."

Don't ever let any researcher overwhelm you with "facts" unless he can prove that these are *all* the facts and that they're 100 percent true. That goes for advertising or any other facet of living, such as civic and social activities. A comedy movie featured a young wife who always got her way by backing her demands with impressive statistics. Asked finally where she got her facts, she said, "I make them up out of my head. As long as I sound positive, it works."

The three leading women's service magazines are constantly battling to prove that each is the best ad medium. Simultaneously each one proclaims that it's leading in *something.*

McCall's, with the top circulation, boasted of the greatest "reach," that is, the biggest total female audience. It cited the Politz Magazine Study.

Ladies' Home Journal emphasized leadership in having the "heaviest buyers"—families with the highest "median income" of the three, with more children per family and more college graduates. Their source was the Daniel Starch Consumer Magazine Report.

Good Housekeeping claimed "editorial and advertising and best buy leadership . . . more editorial pages . . . more advertising pages . . . more service editorial pages." They cited not only Lloyd H. Hall Company's December Hand Count but also challenged: "Check Simmons, Politz, SRDS, Nielsen, BRI." Their ad concluded: "He who graphs last, graphs best!"

But hold on. *McCall's* also advertised "more editorial service linage" than the other magazines and also cited Lloyd

H. Hall Company for the facts and figures in this category. Which one lied—*McCall's* or *Good Housekeeping*? You decide, noting this common trap in research presentations: *Good Housekeeping* claimed "more service editorial *pages*." *McCall's* cited "more editorial service *linage*."

This involves simple arithmetic: As an advertising measurement unit, fourteen "lines" make one inch. In *McCall's*, the average editorial page measured 9⅜ inches × 12⅛ inches, or 680 lines per page. The smaller *Good Housekeeping* page measured 7 inches × 10³⁄₁₆ inches, or 429 lines.

The *Good Housekeeping* graph showed overwhelming leadership in "service editorial" with 947 pages versus *McCall's* 598 pages. But, translating this into linage, *McCall's* took the lead with 406,640 lines to *Good Housekeeping's* 401,973 lines. Both statements were statistically correct depending on which measuring unit was used.

In another instance, two full-page TV ads appeared in the same issue of *The New York Times*. Both heralded results of national Nielsen reports. On page 94, NBC Television Network bragged in large type: "THE BIGGEST AVERAGE NIGHTTIME AUDIENCE." On page 96, CBS Television Network boasted in bold type: **"The biggest average nighttime audience."**

Again it was vital to read the smaller type (advertisers know that comparatively few people do). The NBC claim was "according to the national Nielsen reports for the season to date." The CBS contention was based on "the latest national Nielsen report."

There's one sure conclusion—something is rotten in the state of research usage.

Today's Madison Avenue worship of research and computer data is emphasized by a story told by a realist, A. Edward Miller, former publisher of *McCall's*, now president of Alfred Politz Research: "The UN managed to wire together all of the existing computers in the world to make the most powerful computer setup ever. It took several years to accomplish this incredible task. When it was done, the first question was fed into the machine. It was, 'Is there a God?'

The machine whirred and buzzed for a few seconds and out came the answer—'*Now there is!*' "

Another story tells about the computer that was asked to translate into English the Russian proverb: "Time flies like an arrow." It came up with this line: "Time flies enjoy eating arrows."

Many admen complain that the top echelon genuflect to machines that think, and condemn people who do. Computers can be a great boon; they can also produce profound errors, misconceptions, and lead to outright fraud. The basic flaw is what has been labeled GIGO, meaning Garbage In, Garbage Out. Unless the right facts are fed into the computer, the wrong results will come out—purposely or not.

In a client's conference room, the group awaited the detailed new sales breakdowns provided by their complicated new IBM system. This data, computerized right down to even the smallest towns, would be extremely valuable in judging the effect of advertising expenditure in each little locality instead of by a few big areas as in the past.

The head of research bustled in and proudly handed out duplicated sheafs of figures. Suddenly the sales manager roared, "For God's sake, these figures show that Massillon, Ohio, is selling more product than our best market, Metropolitan New York!" Of course the fault was not with the computer but with the way it had been programmed.

Computers can replace neither the humans who must feed them correctly, nor the human judgment needed to analyze the data. Jacques Barzun suggested: "It will be time to speak of computers as minds, or even brains, when they lay their heads or other parts together to make a man."

Chapter 18

ARE INTERVIEW RESULTS DEPENDABLE?

The Mystery Writers of America ("Crime Does Not Pay . . . Enough") reported in their publication, *The Third Degree,* on a simple survey. A sidewalk researcher in New York City asked passers-by what books they preferred to read from a specified list of paperbacks. The winners were: Shakespeare, the Bible, and a few classics.

After each interviewee answered, the researcher told him to select one of the listed books as a gift to be sent for co-operating. This time the results were different. The book most people selected was *Murder of a Burlesque Queen* by Gypsy Rose Lee. The researcher stated: "The biggest trap you can fall into is believing what people *tell* you they want."

According to an official report, 70.6 million voters cast their ballots in a presidential election. Two weeks later, census interviewers asked "a representative sampling" of people whether or not they voted. According to these answers, 76.6 million people voted.

Something peculiar happens when men and women are asked their views about an action, a problem, a product, or an ad. Most people don't tell what they really think but what they feel they're *supposed* to think. Many individuals will fool even themselves, and consciously or unconsciously lie outright, rather than give an answer which they think reflects low personal standards and taste.

Why do people put up with answering questionnaires that take time and thought? Apparently it's because they want to be "nice." One man answered only one of fifteen questions on a sheet which bore a dime in payment for his answers. He filled in only his age as "over sixty." He added: "I figure that information is about ten cents worth."

A cartoon showed a weary interviewer instructing a housewife at her door: "Just 'Yes,' 'No,' and 'Undecided,' madam. There is no 'Couldn't care less' category."

Increasingly I found people becoming annoyed when, during my years on Madison Avenue, I went door to door, in streets and railway stations, in and outside of stores, interviewing dealers and clerks as well as the public. I was checking mostly on their reactions to advertising campaigns and products. Most people gave me the answers they thought I'd like to hear. They often lied patently rather than appear ignorant; others lied to give a good impression of themselves, and others, as one admitted, "Just to foul up the whole deal."

Jack Griffin, marketing research director of Gerber Products, told a session of the American Marketing Association and the Merchandising Executives' Club of Chicago that while responses to questionnaires "usually make you feel good about your new product, you must learn how to disbelieve their answers."

In a study that asked 500 housewives where they intended to buy toothpaste, 75 percent said "the drugstore." Checking back with those same women later revealed that only 25 percent had bought the toothpaste at the drugstore. Instead, 50 percent of them had purchased it at supermarkets and about 10 percent at discount stores. Apparently they felt in answering the first time that a drugstore sounded like a more fitting place to buy toothpaste.

In checking up on questionnaires, on the spot, I found that some professional interviewers, who are customarily paid poorly, fill in questionnaires themselves. They sometimes write in names out of the directory and from home and apartment mailboxes. Persons long dead have provided live answers on questionnaires.

In spite of all the flaws, research firms, agencies, and advertisers habitually make decisions according to the findings. These become the foundation for advertising expenditures of millions of dollars. On several occasions I've dug out obviously falsified questionnaires filled out in the handwriting of the interviewer, although specified to be filled out by each interviewee personally. Researchers who are confronted with these as evidence of falsification inevitably answer: "Don't worry—our conclusions have been *weighted* to allow for that."

"Weighted? How?"

The glib, mystic answer: "We have our methods."

The "why" of many expensive research projects is a mystery. Coca Cola paid for a check of whether more people would look at an ad featuring empty bottles of Coke or full bottles. What would you figure? The report: 50 percent more looked at the "full-bottles ad" than at the "empty-bottles ad." Apparently it required research dollars to determine that a full bottle will attract more people than an empty bottle.

In a few cases, rugged tycoons still prefer to rely on their own judgment. Some years back, we helped the Mennen Company launch a new after-shave lotion. The agency recommended a light tongue-in-cheek, sex-appeal approach which hadn't been used by a men's lotion up to that time. The proposed ads featured cartoons by R. Taylor and the theme line: "THE MANLY ODOR THAT WOWS THE LADIES!"

All hell broke loose. Various executives wanted different themes. None of them liked the sex-appeal angle. Finally a research outfit was paid to find out what qualities men wanted most in an after-shave lotion. After spending months of precious time and loads of dollars, the report came through: Men wanted such a product to be: 1. Refreshing. 2. Soothing. 3. Healing. The research showed overwhelmingly that men cared absolutely nothing about whether an after-shave lotion's aroma appealed to the fair sex.

The executive staff voted for a "refresh your face" ad campaign. Boss Bill Mennen stared at the report, then tossed it into his "out" tray. He snapped, "Everybody advertises that their lotion is refreshing. Of course no man will admit he gives a damn about sex-appeal in a product. I know that women too like the smell of our lotion. Let's go with 'THE MANLY ODOR THAT WOWS THE LADIES!' "

Within two years, Mennen Skin Bracer rocketed to first place in its field. Men read the amusing ads and tried the product. They liked it and kept buying it—in spite of the opposite research findings.

The Bible of magazine ad ratings is the Starch Magazine Readership Report. Agencies subscribing to this service get regularly researched copies of *Life* magazine, as one example. Each ad of a half page or larger bears a rating for "seen . . . seen/associated . . . read most." All the ads are then rated further on a readers-per-dollar basis, with 100 as the median score.

If your Gimmix ad has a rating of 198–99–63, that means it's almost twice as good in getting readers to "see" it, about average for getting people to "see/associate" it (formerly listed as "read some"), and only 63 percent as good as average for "read most."

With that score, the XYZ Agency brags: "Our Gimmix ad was seen by twice as many readers as the average ad in the magazine!" If challenged on the other figures, they explain: "The only thing that really counts is people *seeing* the ad. After all, if they don't 'see' the ad, nothing else matters."

On the other hand, if the ad had rated 63–99–198, the XYZ research head would boast: "Our Gimmix ad was twice as effective as the average ad in the magazine. The best potential *buyers* are the people who 'read most' of an ad. 'Seeing' is relatively unimportant."

I admired the ability of interviewers to get a woman in her home to leaf through a copy of a thick magazine and rate every ad—until it happened to me. An interviewer called to check me personally on ads in a recent issue of *Printers' Ink,* which has far fewer pages than big consumer magazines. I complied in order to learn at first hand how the system worked.

A young blonde arrived, placed pencil and pad on her enchanting crossed knees, and asked me to go through the magazine page by page. I was to tell her what I had seen, seen/associated or read some, and read most when I'd read the issue originally, a week or two before. I regretfully shifted my eyes and soon found myself thoroughly confused by the questioning after turning a few pages.

Had I seen this ad in this issue, or was it a repeat of one I'd seen in a previous issue? Had I scanned it in *The New York Times* or in *Printers' Ink*? Or was it in *Advertising Age*, or *Sponsor*, or *Anny* (Advertising News of N.Y.)? Had I read "some" of the ad or "most"? Some. No, most. Hell, it was over a week ago—had I really read this issue or flipped through? I was starting to see double and triple. I'd already been at this frustrating exercise for over twenty minutes. I had to prepare for an important conference (they're all "important" in ad alley).

I said unhappily, "I'm afraid I'm giving you many wrong answers."

"Keep going, please. You're doing fine."

"Do you also interview housewives in their homes?"

"Yes. Now if you'll go on to the next page . . ."

"Look—I'm confused—and I'm not even halfway through the magazine. I'm giving many unsure and probably wrong answers. How do your housewives do it?"

She sighed. "The same way you do. Please, let's finish."

"But how about errors—like I'm making?"

Patiently, "Our system is *weighted* against errors."

"How?"

She bit her lip and frowned. "May we proceed—*please*?"

I raced through the remaining pages haphazardly, inaccurately, sputtering a stream of answers.

She arose. "Thank you very much. You've been wonderful."

A special study was conducted by an ad agency. In the current issue of a leading magazine they inserted a few ads which *had not been* in that issue. The ratings reported that the ads which had never appeared had nevertheless been "seen, seen/associated, or read most" by many of the women interviewed.

The results of different measurements are frequently contradictory, as in this example from a popular feature in *Printers' Ink*—"Which Ad Pulled Best?" Comparing two ads in different issues of *McCall's* by Hammond Organ, the report of Starch Ratings stated: "Most people responded to challenge, which is amply demonstrated in ad A (headline: 'SURE YOU CAN') . . . the column of copy in ad B is unpleasantly obtrusive (headline: 'LISTENING-TYPE MUSIC VS. PLAYING-TYPE MUSIC') . . . the overall effect is too busy." Ad A rated over 40 percent higher than ad B in stopping readers.

Each ad bore a coupon. I checked *Printers' Ink* on which ad pulled more coupons. That point, in my experience, is more closely related to sales. The result: Lower-rated ad B "pulled substantially more coupons."

Sam Gill, head of S. E. Gill Associates, told about a "funny strange" survey conducted among 232 men and women in New York City. They were shown a list of twelve magazine names and asked which ones they read regularly—about three of the last four issues. The list: *Argosy, American, Battlefront, Collier's, Cue, Good Housekeeping, Life, Look, McCall's, Que, Woman's Day, Worldbook*. Three were names of magazines that had never existed: *Battlefront, Que,* and *Worldbook;* anyone who said he read any of these three was eliminated from the count.

The results: 9 percent of the remaining interviewees said they regularly read *Collier's*. Asked which of the magazines they'd prefer to keep reading if they had only one, seven percent chose *Collier's*. The payoff: *Collier's* had ceased publication many years before—on January 4, 1957—but nearly one out of ten people in the survey said they were still reading it regularly.

I asked a top agency research head why, in view of errors like this, he and others placed so much credence in the reports. How could they depend on such data for projecting expenditures of millions of dollars annually for their clients? He said, "We realize that the reports may be faulty, but they're the only guide we have."

"Would you use a map of Indiana to take you on a trip through Maine because it's the only guide you have?"

He replied blandly, "One report alone may be erroneous. But a lot of reports together over a period of months make sense."

A man present commented, "It's like the old joke about the fellow who explained that he loses money on every Gimmix he sells. But he makes a profit because he sells so many of them."

Chapter 19

WHICH RESEARCH CAN YOU BELIEVE?

You can't win an argument with the smooth and voluble psychologists of research, the lads with the omnipotent air. Unfailingly they have another obscure answer ready if the preceding obscure answer is questioned.

At a dinner party, a Dr. Glibb (not an M.D.) was providing all the answers about any campaign mentioned. I was telling of a toothpaste ad campaign that had surprised me with its results. "I was sure the theme would flop, but sales were excellent."

"Of course," Dr. Glibb interrupted. "I could have told you without question that it would succeed phenomenally. The theme employed the infallible oral-anal approach."

I continued, "But after a few months the ads lost impact. Sales slumped badly. . . ."

"Naturally, my dear boy, as expected!" Dr. Glibb clarioned. "It had to fail after a bit because, you see, people *change* their thinking in such a case—obviously."

Such razzle-dazzle is generally accepted rather than challenged on Madison Avenue. Also, admen blandly bypass the fact that different research directors and outside organizations often get quite opposite answers on similar projects.

The Ted Bates agency found in surveys that people considered banks cold, austere, and uninterested—not friendly enough. So for their banking client they created a campaign built on the slogan: "You have a friend at Chase Manhattan." They didn't mind resultant gibes such as that there is a

Texan so wealthy that the Chase Manhattan comes to *him* when it needs a friend.

Edward L. Bond, Jr., president of Young and Rubicam, concluded precisely the opposite. His research department, *The New York Times* reported, "carefully analyzed consumers' attitudes toward banks [and] found that banks that try to appear overly friendly lose the respect of their potential customers."

Meadow Brook National Bank steered a middle course. They hired a fashion consultant to transform their women tellers with professional makeup jobs and stylish new dresses. The men sported new blazers. The stylist explained that this was "in accord with a theme of peppy conservatism."

Jack B. Haskins, former manager of advertising research for the Ford Motor Company, and a professor at Indiana University, studied thirteen research reports. His conclusion from this study was that *facts* aren't very important in ads; such components as *emotional* reactions are what influence the public to buy.

Simultaneously, David Ogilvy, head of Ogilvy and Mather International (Number 11), asserted in a TV interview that they'd found ads to be most successful when interesting *factual* information was conveyed to consumers.

A Purina Dog Food campaign was promoted as based on *facts* proving that the product would transform reluctant dogs into "eager eaters." After a few years, apparently new research revealed that people buy dog food not on the basis of facts but are instigated by *emotion*. The new theme emphasized that to please your dog "ALL YOU NEED IS LOVE—AND PURINA."

To make results even more confusing, companies often act to sabotage a competitor's research activities. In one case, new Skis *mint*hol cigarettes were being tested in three markets. Sales reports were very encouraging. Then orders fell suddenly. Investigators were sent hurriedly.

It was discovered that rival makers of established menthol cigarette brands had tracked down the three tests and thrown in heavy extra barrages of local advertising. Special competitive sales crews removed Skis cartons and displays from counters and windows in stores, put up their own. They used free cigarettes and other offers as an inducement. The Skis marketing tests went completely haywire.

This kind of savage attack is not considered unethical by admen and merchandisers. The competitors act not only to confuse testing results—which is one aim—but also to solidify their own sales positions in the markets. They were employing every possible means to keep their own brands from being displaced. "All's fair in love and war" on the Mad Avenue.

Two other cigarette ad campaigns reveal how research data can be disastrously misleading. Various studies concluded that men and women smokers were impressed and influenced positively by a virile, manly image in smoking. Soon two dynamic campaigns exploded. Camels were projected as the "MAN'S CIGARETTE." Alpine advertising challenged: "WHO PUT THE MEN IN MENTHOL? ALPINE!"

Something happened between the answers confirmed by research and the public's purchases of these two brands. The "man's cigarette," Camels, and the Alpine "men in menthol" campaigns fell so fast you could hear the echo of the sales curve dropping.

The following bewilderment occurs time after time: Ageny A spends a client's money on a $100,000 research project and runs campaign A based on it, acclaiming: "Sure-fire big sales increases ahead because campaign based on extensive research!" For whatever reason, sales are not satisfactory. The agency is fired.

Agency B takes over. They use the same research data that the client believes in, perhaps because it cost so much. Also, the admanager had better stand by it or he might be fired for authorizing the expenditure. Out comes campaign B—same research, different interpretation, entirely different theme.

Again salesmen are told: "Sure-fire big sales increases ahead because campaign based on extensive research!" This new ad approach succeeds. The inescapable fact is that the research and the statistics didn't make the difference. A new creative concept did, because it appealed to you, the individual—not you, the statistic.

As a new miracle crutch was needed for multimillion-dollar ad expenditures, researchers reached into the bottomless bag of tricks and came up with "motivational research." Instead of counting noses, this method aimed to reach inside your head and heart to learn what *motivates* you to buy. It's something you're not conscious of yourself, say the motivational wizards.

Do you think you buy brand A cereal because you like the flavor? Anything but. You reach for that package, ma'am, because deep down inside you is buried the erotic desire to race barefoot with some virile playmate through the wheat field pictured on the box.

Advertising Age reported that the Leavitt Corporation in Everett, Massachusetts, marketing River Queen Nuts, "undertook a two-year motivational research project to find the answers" for selling more nuts. Project director Jeanne Schmidt Binstock stated: "There's something almost sinful about nuts, suggesting overindulgence or a reward" and claimed that people therefore develop deeply suppressed guilt feelings about eating nuts.

Research showed, she added, that "People don't think they're good enough for nuts. . . . Everybody's worthy of peanuts, but few consider themselves good enough for cashews." It developed that eaters of cashews consider peanut chewers to be "plebian, dull, unimaginative." The company solution was the merchandising of a River Queen mixture of 55 percent cashews and 45 percent peanuts.

One of the many never-never-land stories told about famed researcher Dr. Ernest Dichter is that he set out to learn what kind of packaging motivated youngsters most. One of his staff gave money to ten "typical American boys" and sent them into a supermarket with instructions to grab the one thing that caught their eye best. Which package won? Each boy came out with a giant watermelon.

Research which proved that most people were motivated toward products with a "youthful image" started a stampede to this theme. Pepsi-Cola claimed to be "for those who think young." Pepsi further encompassed "the young at heart." Quaker State Oil promised to keep cars "running young." Kellogg's Bran Buds ("for regularity") heralded its "youthful new taste."

Admen loved this youth aspect; particularly because a fifteen- to thirty-year-old had about twenty-five more buying years in her carcass than a forty- to fifty-five-year-old. *Redbook* pitched in with an ad campaign proclaiming that "Some girls are too old for *Redbook* . . . eighteen to thirty-four: these are the *Redbook* years." There were some violent reactions. *Redbook* promotion director Milt Franks admitted: "It would seem that we attacked a woman's whole existence when we said she was too old."

So along came contradictory research. *Printers' Ink* reported: "The key fact for marketing men, according to the latest Bureau of Labor Statistics Consumer Spending Study, is that households whose heads are between 25 and 54 purchase at higher rates than do younger families."

Eugene Gilbert, specialist in the youth market, noted that two surveys—nine years apart—showed that younger teen-agers (who would live longer and buy longer than old teen-agers) were fickle. In the second survey of the same youngsters, now adults, only one third bought the same brand they'd preferred nine years before.

On results of a study completed by the Brand Names Foundation, *The New York Times* reported: "Use of certain brands by teen-agers may bar the use by adults of the same brands. . . . Mothers make the buying decisions for many teen-agers for certain products, so that advertising for these products directed at teen-agers would be wasted. . . . Brands used prior to reaching maturity tend to be rejected afterward." Admen pondered—what price youth-appeal now?

A trade magazine headlined a story: "PEPSI GENERATION FIZZLES OUT." Reporting the results of the wild theme—

"COME ALIVE! YOU'RE IN THE PEPSI GENERATION!"—the story went on: "Well, it seems the trouble with the Pepsi generation campaign was that it did everything but sell Pepsi-Cola."

"Research, a great many times, does a great deal more damage than good." Surprisingly, that came from Alfred Politz of the research organization bearing his name. He told the Advertising Writers Association of New York: "If you ask people if they believe what the ad says, you will get a percentage who say yes, sure. Ask if they would bet their life on it and everybody drops out."

Art Buchwald in his column imagined results from a research questionnaire in the early days of America: "Do you think that the Declaration of Independence is a good—or bad—document? Answers: 'Good document 12%. . . . Bad document 14%. . . . No opinion 74%.' A group of those polled felt that the Declaration of Independence had been written by radicals and that the publishing of it at this time would only bring harsher measures from the British."

From another satirist: "It is claimed that in a Gallup Poll to determine the male habits at night the results were tabulated as follows: 10% of the men who get up at night do so to get a drink of water. 15% of the men who get up at night do so to go to the bathroom. The remaining 75% get up to go home."

With its predominating influence, research is not a laughing matter. It has reached the point of such priority in business that one sales manager complained, "Of course sales are down. My men are too busy writing research reports to sell anything."

Some sensible research produces dependable, helpful results. One of the valuable techniques is the "split-run." A publication runs two (or more) different ads for the advertiser in the same spot in alternating copies. Thus a newspaper with 500,000 circulation will print 250,000 of its copies with ad A, and 250,000 copies with ad B. Each ad is in the same position on the same page, and each has the same offer in the body copy or in a coupon.

Here's how it worked in the case of Stern's Nurseries of

Geneva, New York. One ad carried the old headline: "GIANT STRAWBERRIES." The other ad was the same in every detail except for a new headline: "PLUM-SIZE STRAWBERRIES." The latter pulled three times as many orders as the old ad. The test guide proved out in increased sales thereafter for the advertiser, and helped introduce more gardeners to the superior species of strawberries.

Research is a valuable, valid, and often indispensable aid to business. The danger is in overemphasis and over-reliance on the findings. Michael P. Ryan of Allied Chemical Corporation said: "Advertising research is one-half frustration, one-half exclamation point, and one-half question-mark. If this adds up to more than 100 percent, it proves that mathematics and research sometimes give confusing results."

Regardless of research reports, people act according to their personal desires and interests. Research data can't keep up with you because *you keep changing*. You're not sure today how you're going to feel, what you're going to do, how you'll act and react tomorrow. Therefore the research experts can't possibly know. Conditions, feelings, stimuli all change—and you change accordingly. One researcher admitted that people are "as intricate and ever-changing as the weather."

In spite of the overemphasis on research, I have no fear that the Great God Computer-Research will ever displace the need for the creative brain power of the individual. However, an important warning was sounded to business by Peter G. Peterson, president of Bell and Howell, that the danger "is not the science-fiction fear that machines will begin to think like men . . . but that men will begin to think like machines."

Chapter 20

ARE ADMEN SUPERMEN OR SUPER-DUPES?

The confusion caused by questionable research and other uncertain factors contribute to the ulcerous atmosphere that permeates agencies and their dubious "supermen." Are admen, and particularly agencymen, the dominant manipulators they have often been made out to be? What are they really like?

Bernice Fitz-Gibbon, former advertising head at Macy's and Gimbels, explained: "Funny thing, the most creative people in advertising are usually the least screwball. They are non-fey. They are non-whimsey. Good practical salesmen." The same week, while I was chatting with the very conservative president of a giant agency, two of his creative people, a copy chief and an art director, walked by. Both sported beards and almost shoulder-length hair. The boss told me, "Screwballs—I hate 'em! But most of our best creative people are nuts."

One thing most agencymen have in common is *fear*—based on the uncertainty of keeping an account, holding a job. An executive called advertising "the most exciting industry existing today. The most insecure industry existing today."

You can smell this fear when you enter a conference room. You can see it in the stony or falsely smiling faces, the staring or shifting eyes. You can hear it in the braggard voice and the uncertain stutter of the unsure. Often this fear is based on the individual's lack of ability, which frequently masquerades as overconfidence.

The more assured the adman appears on the outside, the more fearful he may be within. The steely eye, the out-thrust chin, the purposeful stride, often are camouflage for a frightened spirit cringing behind the bold façade. These men often are unscrupulous, with a perverted sense of business morality caused by fear. As Robert Frost stated: "The people I am most scared of are the people who are scared."

A note in an advertising trade magazine says: "Sullivan, Stauffer, Colwell & Bayles . . . 'readjusted' its personnel lineups following the switch . . . 30 persons were given one-day notice of their dismissal from the agency." The adman never knows when the axe will fall.

Every week in *Advertising Age,* an eagerly scanned listing of "Advertising Agency Personnel Changes" appears. Dozens upon dozens of names are printed weekly. It's doubtful that any other business begins to match the horrendous job turnover rate. Chief Norman H. Strouse at J. Walter Thompson said that the past year's total turnover was 32 percent (the industry average is believed to be about 25 percent), with one in six of those paid over $15,000 "on the move each year."

A survey by Corwin Consultants, an "executive search" firm, summed up ad jobs as: "Too fast up. Too fast down." Seventy percent of the admen they checked had changed jobs in the last two years. Many had held up to six or seven jobs on Madison Avenue and were *not* senior citizens. The admen's complaints included "too much backbiting and politicking . . . amoral behavior of power-mad top executives . . . too addicted to fads . . . too little originality, too much me-too . . . more phonies and nuts per square inch than most businesses."

Lou Hagopian, executive at N. W. Ayer and Son (Number 16), involved in his agency's loss of the $28 million Plymouth account, said: "Unless you own the business you're going to get fired some day." It's almost inevitable. It's the name of the game. Said artist Tom Frank, who went from Ayer to

Young and Rubicam for one month, then left: "The advertising business is a great business of compromise, but you compromise the wrong things—your peace of mind, health, sanity."

One day a friend representing one of the leading magazines sought my advice on which person to see in our agency on a big account. "I called on Jack Doe and Dick Roe last month. I was told that they're not here any more."

"They were dumped a couple of weeks ago. The account's sales aren't doing well because the product is behind the times. So, of course, the first step was to blame the guys handling the account. In charge now are Steve Boe and Tom Toe, but don't count on them being here very long."

He pulled out a little worn black book listing the names of people he called on at various agencies. He turned to our agency page. Under a long column of crossed-out names he drew heavy lines through the last two. The opposite page listing another agency had as many crossed-out names.

"All your pages like that?"

He nodded. "It's frightful!" He flipped page after page filled with cross-outs. "I feel like an executioner, drawing lines through the names of the guillotined. Accounts and jobs turn over so fast, I never know who's coming or going in this stinking rat race. More people are wiped out on Madison Avenue each month than when I was in Korea in its worst days."

A newsletter reported that Charles Brower, president of Batten, Barton, Durstine and Osborn (Number 4), investigated setting up a retirement pension plan at age sixty-five. Checking showed that he and Bruce Barton were the only qualified candidates from about 8,000 employees.

A newspaper item about a wide network personnel "realignment" stated: "Comment on the NBC cast changes was muted . . . if only because as a group TV presidents seldom are in office long enough to appeal to students of executive geriatrics. The only personality with tenure in TV, one executive quipped, is the plasterer who prepares old offices for new tenants."

Why so much turnover? Part of it is due to the great number of changes in accounts, as advertisers switch from one agency to another. Agency changes total over 20 percent a year. In one year, the changes in the top eleven accounts involved over $75 million. There were altogether about 250 account changes listed.

Included in account changes in one year were budgets as high as: Gillette Company, $25 million; General Foods, $15 million; Alberto-Culver, $15 million; Philip Morris, $15 million. Since hundreds of people may be required to work on an account the size of Gillette, for example, hundreds of people may be fired from the agencies that lose the accounts. The agency that gets an account usually must hire more people to service it, unless they have recently lost an account of about the same size—which happens.

It's not unusual that some of the people in an agency which lost the account are hired to work on it by the agency which gets the account. This makes a curious kind of Madison Avenue logic. People are hired as "experienced" on the account, specifically experienced in helping to produce the kind of apparently unsatisfactory advertising that lost the account in the first place.

John F. Kennedy told a story about "experience," a hallowed word in ad alley. Accused by Richard Nixon during the presidential campaign of lack of experience, he observed: "I know a banker who served thirty years as president of a bank. He had more experience, until his bank went broke, than any other banker in Massachusetts. But if I ever go into the banking business, I do not plan to hire him."

The changeover of accounts was called a "sickening spectacle" by an agency head who is noted for snatching accounts from others. This no-holds-barred struggle to get accounts away from other agencies is the root of many evils.

The ad press is filled with rumors, true or false, such as: "A reliable source revealed that the Gimmix Corporation is seeking a new outfit to replace their current PDQ Agency." Immediately other agencies start ringing the phone at Gimmix. They stumble over each other to make a presentation.

PDQ executives race over to the Gimmix offices in desperation—to kill or confirm the rumor. Dozens of persons on the Gimmix account at PDQ start "putting out feelers" for new jobs as they worry that the rocking ship will sink.

Even if there is no basis for the rumor, such a situation may cause trouble between account and agency. Wooed by costly lunches at posh restaurants by eager agencies, softened by front-row seats to hit shows, the Gimmix admanager starts wondering if he shouldn't consider a new agency "for the good of the company."

Poor old PDQ—which would cut another agency's throat just as ruthlessly, and had entertained just as lavishly in seeking the account—loses the Gimmix business. Now the back-stabbers really go to work. Sounding serious, secretive, sure, they arrange dates with other advertising clients on the PDQ roster. Over martinis and filet mignon, they mention, "I had a tip that two more accounts are leaving PDQ in the next few weeks. They'll lose twelve million more in billing, along with some of their best people. They're slipping fast. Too bad they're not a more creative shop—like us. You can't afford second-rate stuff these days. Now in our agency. . . ."

Under such pressure, even the most loyal clients become uneasy. Like others, they don't want to be with a losing team. They start picking flaws in the work PDQ has been doing for them. Exit PDQ, like many another agency that has been scuttled by false rumors.

In addition to shifts of accounts, much job turnover is also due to incompetence. There's an excess of "charm boys" in agencies, along with svelte, sexed-up career women (in addition to the sound, hard workers). Most of the men enter the field because of its glamor and high salaries. They get by primarily on the basis of looks and social graces as they work hard at being pleasant and entertaining. They may not be intellectual companions, but they dress up publicity photos, luncheon tables, and conference rooms.

Their trademarks are the he-man grip of hands, the grim visage and stalwart nod of head when agreeing with the client or agency bosses. Knowing very little else, they do know how to put up a front, to appear brainy, and above all to exude absolute confidence, no matter how unsure they may be.

Their prime ability, one not to be minimized, is the shrewd knack for using the brains of others to make up for their own lack of creative, administrative, and other abilities. That coupled with ruthless ambition and assertion in taking credit for the ideas and efforts of others, form an unbeatable combination—for a while. This kind of individual attains a kind of celebrity as "a person who is known primarily for his well-knownness."

These phonies produce a baffling phenomenon. They are fired from one large agency after another, frequently getting new and more important positions each time, *at increasing salaries*. Here's how the process works, year in, year out:

The first and essential step is to get a job, no matter how small, at one of the biggest agencies or advertisers—for example, at Young and Rubicam or Procter and Gamble. Fired for incompetence after a year or more, the individual practices an air of great confidence and authority, the look that says, "Here comes a man's man!"

Having mastered this pose and rehearsed his lies, he applies to J. Walter Thompson (Number 1) in this case. He lies brazenly, convincing the personnel interviewer that he had a far more important job at Young and Rubicam than he actually held. He may have been a glorified messenger boy but says he was an account executive. He is hired at a higher salary because of that loftier status. His precious asset is "Young and Rubicam (or Procter and Gamble) experience."

Thompson brags in turn that they've added knowledge acquired at Y & R to their own. It usually takes about two years for the big agency to discover that the higher-salaried man is a fraud. They fire him. His inadequacy may have been camouflaged by the number of bodies and red tape in a giant company.

Now Gregory Q. Phony approaches and is hired by Batten, Barton, Durstine and Osborn because he can be introduced to clients as bringing BBDO, Y & R, and J. Walter experience.

He is gaining his finest hours. He continues on from job to bigger job. He never admits that he was fired. He alibis, "I'm a man on my way up. The other agencies didn't fully appreciate me. They didn't give me a chance to use my maximum abilities and achieve my full potential."

If asked why he only lasted at each agency for two years or so, he states shamelessly, "I'm not a floater—I'm a fast mover. I couldn't wait for a conservative agency to take years to move me up to the next stage where I belonged." Another favorite ploy of the executive who is fired for incompetence: "I quit because the only place left for me to go was the top job—and that was taken."

As the climber adds agency names to his experience record he's also adding impressive client names, the biggest. He can rattle off contact with loads of gilt-edge companies—General Foods, Ford, Reynolds Tobacco, the greatest. It's overlooked that he was yanked off one account after another for lack of ability.

The agencies who fired the phony rarely tell the truth when asked for references. There are two reasons: 1. This would reflect on their own hiring abilities and personnel standards. 2. They enjoy knowing that a recommendation will get the man hired so that he can mess things up for the competitive agency in his new job.

Comedian Lou Holtz told a classic story about a glutton who would eat his fill in a restaurant then say he had no money to pay the check. He was always let off when he promised that he would do the same to a competitor the next night.

Dominated by selfish fear, personnel people usually prefer to bypass the fact that a man was bounced from agency to agency and that they may be hiring a rolling stone. If the head man asks, "Why the hell did you hire that lamebrain?" —after the employee flops—there is a ready, righteous alibi: "He worked for Y & R, BBDO, and J. Walter. I'm not to blame for hiring a man with that background."

Another reason for job insecurity on Madison Avenue is the lack of loyalty to long-time employees when a new department head is brought in. A chilling example is this big-space ad in a trade magazine: "Creative Vice-President [wanted]. This is your opportunity to take charge of the creative department of a growing agency that bills over 10 million in consumer accounts. If you like our copy and art people (and we believe you will), keep them. If not, you can get rid of any one of them. Or all of them. . . ."

The new creative vice president may well be one of the phonies with a string of big-agency credits in his background. If so, he may very likely come in and make a clean sweep of employees just to show he's boss and that the others "are not up to my standard—they're strictly second-raters."

Because they're well aware of their own inadequacies, such men are usually fearful and frantic. They're quick to perpetrate offensive, fraudulent advertising to try to get sales and save their own skins. Many betray their insecurities on the psychoanalyst's couch, or more often across a bar. They contribute to advertising's unusually high percentage of alcoholics and near-alcoholics.

A popular definition of the well-adjusted Emergency Avenue adman is one whose intake of pep pills just overbalances his intake of tranquilizers long enough to enable him to get to his psychoanalyst's office each session.

Dr. Marvin A. Block, chairman of the American Medical Association's Committee on Alcoholism and Narcotics, said that advertising executives are a breed apart, the "Delta type who drink steadily all day long." Describing the typical day of a two-fisted adman with a glass in each fist, he said, "He has a few drinks on the train, and then a quick one before going to the office. He drinks his lunch—three or four martinis. In the afternoon, he goes down for a pack of cigarettes and has a quick one." That's just a start. . . .

"After work, he has a drink or two with the boys, then a few on the train, and then a couple of cocktails with his wife. He may have wine with his dinner, then, of course, a few highballs after dinner and a nightcap."

Part of the adman's problem (most are *not* drunks) is the

midday liquid lunch break, headlined in *The New York Times* as "ADVERTISING: LUNCH IS A TIME FOR BUSINESS." The story stated that "To a substantial segment of the advertising fraternity the daily 'business lunch' is . . . a way of life. . . . Lunch begins at 12 and ends at 3, and during that three-hour period things happen. Contacts are made, offers tendered and deals closed."

"Personal contacts" are of top importance in advertising as in other businesses. Over good food and drinks—the more the friendlier—agencymen, clients, media, and other salesmen get to know each other, take their hair down, get vital okays. The choice of the right restaurant, then the right table, the right item on the menu—all are significant in the pursuit of the Big Dollar.

It is said about many an adman, "Don't see him after lunch—he may act conscious but he's really blind and deaf if not dumb." I recall a meeting with an admanager at 3 P.M. He sailed in from a liquid lunch at 3:20, sat swaying slightly in his chair, his eyes blurry. Asked whether he'd rather postpone the meeting, he blurted angrily, "Why, g'damnit?"

He finally okayed one ad for immediate production as we were on deadline due to his persistent delaying tactics. A week and thousands of dollars later, we brought the new color photograph and complete ad down in the *morning* for his approval. He raged, "You never even showed me this ad before. Your agency can tear up the whole thing and pay the costs."

His assistant said, "I heard you okay the ad last Thursday, Mr. Lush."

We were off the hook. The assistant was fired. It might easily have been the agency that was given the boot.

Many top business executives distrust agency people, the endless reams of memoranda, and advertising itself. In the accounting department, two and two always add up to four. In the advertising department, two and two are often expected to add up to fourteen. Why? Partly because there's no set rule of thumb for advertising results. Partly because admen are likely to create purposeful confusion and also promise too much lest they undermine the client's belief in their abilities and in the exaggerated power of advertising.

The story is told that the chairman of the board of one of the nation's largest corporations complained: "I know positively that half of our advertising expenditure is wasted. The trouble is—I don't know which half."

Analysis makes the answer come clear: The "half" which is wasted, inefficient, and harmful to advertisers and the public, emphasizes the use of the half-truth, the exaggerations, the asinine, and the fraudulent in creating advertising. Most of the wasteful "half" stems from the incompetence, bluff, and insecurity flourishing in the field. Add to these faults the harassments of feverish cut-throat competition. All combine to blur and distort the agency-eye view of seeing and serving the public *and* business best.

Chapter

THE UNKINDEST CUT— CUT-THROAT COMPETITION

21

"In new business, if you engage in anything short of a direct assault on the jugular vein, you're in the Mickey Mouse league. It's true of any selling—if you don't have or can't develop a killer instinct, you shouldn't get into the ring." That realistic advice was addressed to the Magazine Advertising Sales Club by William E. Holden, executive vice president of Fuller and Smith and Ross.

It is not unusual for twenty or more agencies to engage in a scramble to snare an account that may be "on the loose." The gamble, involving costly investment in time, money, and energy—frequently to the detriment of the agency's overall operations and current clients—bears the same sudden death risk as backing a new Broadway play. In the theater, if the critics turn thumbs down on opening night, the play and the entire investment, along with shattered hopes, may be gone the next day.

When a big advertiser announces his selection, all the competing agencies except the winner are stone dead. The weeks and months of preparation are for nothing. But most admen are resilient, optimistic, and indefatigable. A rejected adman shrugged off the defeat: "One good thing about not getting the account, we'll never have to worry about losing it."

In print and verbally, agency heads state repeatedly about going after new accounts: "We never make a speculative presentation. We consider it unethical." But as soon as a big account opens the door a crack, the same agency storms in with a speculative presentation which may cost tens of thousands of dollars.

In a rare moment of truth, the president of an important agency explained after too many cocktails how they go after new business: "We decide what accounts we want. We list them as targets for study and attack. Whether we think the advertising they're getting is good or bad has little to do with it. The account that's getting poor advertising is more vulnerable, but we welcome the toughies too. For instance, here's how we landed the Gimmix Company." He named a leading advertiser. "It illustrates our usual system."

He held up one finger. "The first step is to arrange an appointment with one of the top Gimmix executives—the advertising head, or preferably the chairman or president. This is usually fairly easy because we say that 'we just want to get acquainted.' Or we find someone who's close to the key Gimmix man one way or another. He sees that we're granted an interview 'as a courtesy.' "

He held up two fingers. "Now the door is open. Our first visit is just 'exploratory.' Maybe we tell the agency story, maybe we don't. We have one prime objective in that first meeting: *Before we leave, we must plant at least one tiny seed of discontent with his current agency in the advertiser's mind.*"

He finished his drink and signaled to the waiter for another. "How do we accomplish that? We point out some of the services we're giving others that we've learned he's not getting. No, we don't mention that we charge for such extras. We ask how he's doing in what our investigations have revealed is his weakest market. We *happen* to mention the rating of a client's TV show which is double that of his best program (of course we don't speak of our own low-rated shows). There are a dozen weaknesses to inflame, if you look for them with destruction in mind."

He winked as he gulped his fresh on-the-rocks. "We solidify our new friendly relationship with Gimmix executives. Lots of expensive entertaining, naturally. Gradually we fertilize the seeds of discontent to grow into vigorous doubts. It may take anywhere from months to years. The effort and long wait are worthwhile when gunning for millions of dollars in billing, right?"

"Well—"

"When discontent has grown into flourishing dissatisfaction, we nudge the prospect into outright animosity against his current agency. That's when we attack with a full-blown presentation and land the account." (Agency head Carl Ally told a class at the New School for Social Research: "The trouble with most new-business presentations is—it's a form of organized lying.")

"All's fair with this procedure"—the president's smile was a barricuda's—"because we know that other agencies—including the one we're knifing—are trying to cut our throats similarly on our accounts."

He concluded, "That's the name of the game—constant cut-throat competition. Loss of accounts is inevitable. Our only protection is to gun for the other fellow's accounts mercilessly. I don't know of one sizable agency in the U.S., probably not in the world, which can brag that it has never lost an account, whether through its own faults or being shot down by another agency's attack."

Sooner or later, every agency sends an announcement to the press that it has "resigned the account because of basic policy differences," or similar oblique wording. That's usual Madavenese for: *"We've been dumped."* Typical from *The New York Times:* "The following is a release, in its entirety, that was received yesterday: 'The Blank Advertising Agency of New York and Newark, New Jersey, has notified its good client, maker of Blank-Blank Food Products, of its desire to terminate a relationship limited by basic marketing and advertising differences.' "

If the foregoing report of the cold-blooded chase seems exaggerated (though reported verbatim from the agency president's mouth), this further example is illustrative: Probably no ad campaign has been lauded as much as the job done for Volkswagen by Doyle Dane Bernbach (Number 8). However, addressing the Sales Executives Club, Paul R. Lee, then merchandising director for Volkswagen, mildly criticized one ad produced by DDB. The following day calls poured in from rival agencies seeking his account.

Exasperated, Mr. Lee stated: "It's a poor reflection on our business that you can't make a friendly criticism without producing this sort of reaction."

In a news release, Frank S. Owens, advertising manager for Utica Club Beer, stated that the Benton and Bowles campaign had created a great deal of favorable comment and helped build sales to an all-time high. He added that the agency had just been fired. A brand new "hot creative agency," Wells, Rich, Greene, Incorporated, was appointed. President of B & B William Hesse commented: "Often in this wonderful business of ours, decisions are based on the search for the pot of gold at the end of the rainbow. They may not be rational, good business decisions. . . ."

A top executive of one of the biggest agencies put it in this blunt way: "A hot young agency, like a hot tomato, has more guys chasing her than an older, more sophisticated dame, even though the older one may give you a better time."

An agency that adds several accounts in a short period is labeled "a hot soup." Usually they gain further business that they wouldn't have added otherwise, deserved or not. Typical announcement in *The New York Times:* "Tussy Cosmetics will switch its $1.1 million account to Richard K. Manoff, Inc. from the Kudner Agency. . . . This is the agency's second acquisition this week—the other being the $500,000 Ronrico Puerto Rican Rum account."

If Manoff listed another sizable account in the next week, it would be called "hot" and make exceptional strides. If Kudner dropped another account or two quickly, it would be tabbed "a loser." Panic could set in, with further severe losses. That happened when the agency lost the tremendous Buick account. As soon as the news broke, the wolves were at a dozen doors as admanagers of other Kudner accounts started receiving those ingratiating phone calls for lunch, dinner, and the theater.

Kudner, which had been one of the top agencies, started slipping badly. It was eventually merged to become Tatham-Laird and Kudner, well below the "top twenty" position it had once rated.

The ceaseless search for the slightest opening to try to pirate an account is illustrated by this popular story of adman meeting adman:

"You knew Harry Bloops, the account supervisor and veep at Norman, Craig and Kummel, formerly at Ketchum-MacLeod and Grove, right?"

"Sure. Great guy. The greatest. A pal. What about him?"

"He dropped dead this morning."

"That's awful. Terrible. What did he have?"

"I think it was a heart—"

"No, no—I mean—what accounts did he have?"

Chapter

COMMON KNIFE-IN-THE-BACK TECHNIQUES

22

A survey of agencymen's attitudes included the question: "Would you want your son to go into advertising?" One replied, "No. He might try to steal my accounts."

If a man can "put an account in his pocket"—get so close to an advertiser that he may shift the account along with himself to most any agency of his choice—he can write his ticket at most shops. Particularly, if it's a prestige account, one that looks good in the ad news columns, agencies will pay him a huge salary to join them, vying with others, even though they're left with only a slight profit or perhaps a break-even at the start.

The heads of the new agency then often try in every possible way to undermine the man who brought in the account. If they in turn can gain control, he can't take it away at will. They can then also reduce his "take." That's considered fair on Madison Avenue because most every account supervisor is trying to win over the agency's accounts for himself. Then he could move out with an account or several for a bigger salary and percentage for himself elsewhere—and to hell with loyalty to the agency.

Various executives at the same agency keep knifing others for their own advantage. Frequently the client becomes bewildered and then disgusted. In one case, scrappy partners A and B joined agency C, after dissolving their own company and bringing in a multimillion-dollar account.

Instead of producing harmony, new frictions developed. A

and B each tried to gain dominance on the account. Meanwhile president C was striving to win the client's loyalty for the agency, behind the backs of A and B.

Finally at a lunch meeting alone with the client, A went too far in criticizing his former partner. Returning to his office, the disturbed client phoned B and told B what had happened. B rushed over and said that A was not only a rat but was so inept and undependable that he should be booted off the account.

Both A and B took their complaints separately to president C. As soon as they left, C dashed over to convince the client that the most important factor for him was not the services of either A or B, both dispensable, but of C. The client absorbed it. Then he appointed agency D which had nothing at all to do with A, B, or C.

Another facet of agency operations is the relentless pursuit by individuals of bigger and better titles. This side issue takes the executive's eye further from what should be the main objective of producing the most effective advertising. A *New York Times* study of titles on Madison Avenue reported: "Where once there were only vice presidents, today there are literally dozens of delicate gradations to distinguish the troops from the generals."

Benton and Bowles hasn't just a chairman at the head. The McKittrick Directory of Advertisers in its agency edition noted an honorary chairman, a founder chairman, and an ordinary chairman.

Ted Bates and Company listed an honorary chairman of the board, a chairman of the board, two vice chairmen of the board, and a president running a poor fifth. Once the president of a company was the head man in every way. Today if the president is not also the "chief executive officer," he may have less power than many vice presidents.

J. Walter Thompson, as the world's largest agency, listed 140 vice presidents plus four executive vice presidents and eight senior vice presidents.

Snaring the Big Title is no minor matter to admen. One

agency vice president resigned and took millions of dollars in billing (his "vest-pocket account") over to a rival agency. His reason: Three other men whom he considered beneath him were promoted to senior vice presidencies while he was passed by. He said, "Being just a lousy plain vice president in an agency today is like being the men's room attendant."

At one time, thumbing its nose at the field, Freeman and Gossage listed five officials as "presidents." Later they named a tiny Chinese-American woman as their only president. The others can all now refer to themselves until eternity as ex-presidents.

A small company appointed as honorary vice president a stray *dog* because: "His ability to get along with anyone, his prompt response to a pat on the back, his interest in watching others work, his great knack for looking wise and saying nothing, make him a natural."

Other companies in various branches of advertising have hugged the title trend. A listing showed NBC with fifty-one vice presidents, CBS with forty-five, ABC with forty-seven—a total of 143 network vice presidencies. New combinations of titles are born daily. NBC had a senior executive vice president, qualifying as a vice president's vice president.

It becomes rather complicated. An ad column reported: "Marvin Corwin, who has resigned as senior vice president and plans director in charge of media, research and marketing for Doyle Dane Bernbach, Inc. . . . will become president and chief operating officer of Erwin Wasey, Inc. . . . [which] has just had its name shortened from Erwin, Wasey, Ruthrauff & Ryan, Inc., a member of the Interpublic Group of Companies, Inc."

Madavenuers love to have their names on the agency letterhead. That accounts for such unwieldy appellations as Campbell, Emery, Haughey, Hutchinson and Lutkins, Incorporated. Partly it makes sense as clients like to be served by a "partner." Much of it is due to the urge for self-aggrandizement.

I was president of an agency called Kiesewetter, Baker, Hagedorn and Smith. Previously, Mr. Kiesewetter, the founder, had made partners of Mr. Wetterau, the head of art, and myself, creative chief then. The agency name became Kiesewetter, Wetterau and Baker. Col. Lemuel Q. Stoopnagle wired me: "With all the 'wet' in there, the name should be Kiesewetter, Wetterau & *Blotter*."

An admanager used to introduce his luncheon host proudly to table-hoppers as "Joe Okes, vice president of J. Walter." That's fast becoming passé. If the admanager isn't served by at least a senior vice president, he may feel slighted.

Actually the "advertising manager" himself may now only be the bag carrier for the real advertising manager. The latter has generally been retitled vice president in charge of advertising or director of advertising or director of advertising and public relations or director of marketing and advertising.

Admen often don't know whom to butter up or snub, because of title confusion. At an industry luncheon, I was seated next to a client at my left who was the big power in his sizable firm. Still he kept his lowly v.p. title. The rival agencyman at my right whispered, "I used to know that guy. How does he rate now?" I answered, "Oh, he's still just a vice president."

The disappointed adman shook his head sadly. He called out to my companion patronizingly, "Hi, how you doin', kid?" If he'd known that the man controlled a million-dollar ad budget, he'd have been over there sitting in his lap—and cutting my throat.

Titles have considerable market value. When the man who was senior vice president switches jobs he can generally add thousands to his salary. It makes a vital difference if he can say that he was one of the eight senior vice presidents at J. Walter Thompson rather than one of the 140 plain vice presidents.

Every time a Madavenuer adds a title he can get a listing in the trade press, and probably a photograph. Since advertisers and agencymen devour the ad news columns, a mention may be worth many dollars in the marketplace.

Perhaps Fred Allen started the clamor for a switch from plain vice president to more impressive variations with his bruising definition. He described a vice president as a man who comes in every morning to find a molehill on his desk—and spends the rest of the day making it into a mountain. The *Wall Street Journal* noted that ulcers are the result of mountain-climbing over molehills.

The prevalent ulcers are also induced by those advertisers who use their head-chopping, agency-firing power in cruel, often seemingly insane ways. Most admen painfully bear it. Rosser Reeves, as head of Ted Bates, said: "I'm chairman, so I haven't a boss in the agency—but I have dozens of bosses—every client is my boss!"

A gracious, attractive adwoman who was applying to me for a job told why she'd left a high-paying agency position: "I was assigned to one of the top cosmetic accounts, a notorious agency-killer. At my first meeting in their offices, about twenty people were present. Finally the boss entered. As I was introduced to him, I smiled. He glared at me, then started to address the group. Suddenly he stopped, then said to me in a loud voice, 'You have the ugliest mouth I've ever seen on a woman!' "

She shuddered. "I shriveled. I realized that this was his way of telling the others and me that I was just another doormat. I put up with many such indignities but finally had to quit. I think I aged ten years in those twelve months on the account."

Another ruthless advertising tycoon is quoted as saying in an office conference, "I consider the high-salaried men and women on my staff, and the agency executives who serve me, as *prostitutes*. Only the big money makes them put up with me. I squeeze everything I can out of them until I'm ready to throw them away."

This kind of advertiser caused an agencyman to comment bitterly, "One thing you gotta say for the account, nobody in his right mind will ever want to take it away from us." But agencymen on the scent of a vulnerable account are seldom in their "right mind."

An agency head cited as a most desirable client "a guy you can work with who won't have contempt for you and for whom you won't have contempt. There's a lot of contempt in this business."

The "what have you done for me lately?" syndrome is standard procedure. An agency may score triumphs for the client but can usually expect little lasting praise or loyalty. If a few things go wrong, or if no dramatic new accomplishments are recorded, their position may become shaky overnight.

The same goes for agency employees. A man may land a $5 million account, or create a tremendously successful campaign theme, but the pressure is always on: *"What have you done for us lately?"* Each man knows that other agency executives are constantly trying to pull him down and climb up over him. The bigger his title, the more ruthless the competitive back-stabbing.

The bloody wars escalate to new heights, or depths. Some years back, spotlighting fierce agency competition, an ad magazine ran the cartoon caption: "The building's cleaning women are making a fortune selling the wastebasket contents of one agency to another." Soon some agencies, alerted by the cartoon, sent around office memos warning employees not to discard carbons of important memos, copy, and such in wastebaskets.

Now, to fit the need, agencies can buy a destroyit Electric Wastebasket for only $99. It weighs thirteen pounds and chews up the papers thrown in, transforming them into eighth-inch strips. It has already been suggested that another electrical contraption may follow, for sale to frustrated agency spies. The new device would piece the eighth-inch strips back into their original readable form.

You can't dream up anything so wild or impossible that it hasn't happened in the normal functioning of Madison Avenue—or will.

Chapter

THE MYTH OF THE OMNIPOTENT ADMAN

23

An adman could, if he would, tell about astounding mistakes made by "omnipotent" advertisers and agencymen, like the following. When Mrs. Patricia Winter, originator of House of Herbs products, was just out of her teens, decades ago, her physician/father produced a substance for patients who had exceptional problems with excess perspiration and odor. She packed a batch of the stuff in jars. Friends who tried it were delighted with results.

She decided to approach an advertising agency to recommend it to a client as a brand new kind of product. After a meeting in the plush Madison Avenue offices of one of the largest agencies, she was told—with a notable lack of interest—that they would consider the matter: "Don't call us, we'll call you." Some time later, she was advised by mail by an agency executive that no market could be developed for deodorant products. Their findings convinced them that enough people couldn't possibly be interested in anything to combat perspiration odor.

Not awed in the least by the giant agency's turndown, Pat kept trying. She sold the product directly to a cosmetic company. They marketed it as a brand still popular today. She collected lots of royalty checks which outweighed the Madison Avenue rejection considerably. It is estimated that over $130 million in advertising is expended annually on deodorants. The agency had erred more than slightly.

In spite of the best-laid plans and the most expert know-how that money can buy, advertising sales potential and results too often come a cropper even among the largest advertisers. General Mills found this out with its snack products euphemistically named Bugles, Whistles, and Daisy*s, as reported in *Printers' Ink.*

Every detail was tested exhaustively, including the names. Tubes and Horns lost out. Daisy*s (which someone referred to as "rejected Cheerios") won over Buttercups.

The advertising campaigns and test marketing were conducted meticulously in a number of markets over a period of not just a few weeks but extending from two months to over two years. In each case, as soon as the products and advertising were introduced in each market, people fell all over each other in grabbing the packages off store shelves.

But as the promising products were advertised nationally, *Printers' Ink* stated: ". . . an alarming truth began to show up. Yes, indeed, consumers rushed to their local supermarkets, clamoring and shouting for Whistles, Bugles and Daisy*s. . . . They bought them, they tried them, then, apparently, they went right back to their potato chips and onion soup dip . . . initial trial was fantastic; repeat business was something less than that . . . disappointing . . . volume has not been as high as the company was led to expect. . . ."

Can admen sell *children* against their wishes, if not adults? Trying it leads to madness and disaster, as admen (and parents) know too well.

A research expert, Gene Reilly, sent his human computers out to homes to question kids about their likes and dislikes. He reported: "We discovered that the child five through eight years old . . . has opinions and is not too shy to express them." Most any parent could have stated that without it costing an investigating cent.

On one of the tape-recorded interviews, an eight-year-old gurgled, "Sure I'd heard that M & M's don't melt in your hand [like they show on TV], but a friend of mine and I tried holding them a long time and they finally got squishy. So I guess they do melt if you wait long enough." Ten thousand M & M commercials can never convince that youngster and his friends otherwise.

Reilly discovered further that kids are "discriminatory," as another child's tape voice revealed: "I think if I had to choose between Wise and Lay's potato chips, I'd take Lay's. They taste a little better and they don't have as much salt. . . ." Imagine asking that kid further, "But you said you liked Wise's TV commercials better?" and the youngster replying nasally, "Yeah, but they got too much salt."

Corn Products Company spent millions of dollars year after year—over $2 million in some years—airing this catchy jingle for Bosco Chocolate-Flavored Milk Additive:

> "I love Bosco,
> It's rich and choc'lat-y.
> Momma puts it in my milk
> Because it's good for me."

After a while, reports started coming in from all over the nation that were rather disturbing to the advertiser. The favorite song heard in school playgrounds and wherever the kids gathered was:

> "I hate Bosco,
> It's full of T.N.T.
> Momma puts it in my milk
> To try to poison me."

More millions of dollars in advertising muscle couldn't persuade kids to change their tune. The jingle was dropped.

Many advertising failures have been traced to trying too hard to sell people until they became fed up and deserted the product. At a marketing seminar, Byron Osterwell, vice president of Lippincott and Margulies, designers, pointed to holiday liquor decanters as an example of "too attractive" packaging.

He said: "The first one you buy, you find some use for, such as refilling it with vinegar or olive oil. By the time you've got three or four, you're complaining, 'What are these damned decanters doing around the house?' But you feel guilty about throwing them away because they're so pretty. So you wind up switching brands and buying your liquor in the ordinary, plain, undistinguished bottles you're accustomed to."

Gauge people's reactions in advance? How—when the individuals can't predict their own responses?

Speaking to advertisers, not to the public, the same expert noted that even the biggest and smartest companies have made packaging mistakes—whoppers. Such a "near-infallible" company as Procter and Gamble, as he put it, placed a lot of faith and dollars behind Gleem in aerosol cans. It was a "resounding failure." Admen still can't figure why you'll go for shaving cream in aerosol cans but turn down toothpaste in a similar package.

Also, advertisers—no matter how large and dominating—have learned from bitter experience that one success doesn't provide the magical key to the public pocketbook. International Latex Company scored great successes with women's girdles, then with baby pants, and other items. When they confidently produced a line of baby oil and powder, they flopped miserably. One enormous flaw in their planning—which any young mother could have spotted—was the use of gaudy, gleaming packages. Such designs had great appeal for fashions but they were appallingly bad for products to apply to baby's delicate skin.

Can advertising success be guaranteed? Agency president William Bernbach gave the answer unequivocally: "Anyone who says he's sure a campaign will be a success is a phony." That spotlights the high percentage of phonies on Madison Avenue as innumerable agencymen assure clients: "This campaign is certain to be a triumph—it can't miss." How else can he get the advertiser's okay?

The cleverest campaigns can't beat down your resistance if the ads rub you the wrong way, as Mr. Bernbach too has learned. Probably Doyle Dane Bernbach has the highest batting average for successes. To sell Four Roses Whiskey, they created a campaign based on the theme that you only had to pay a few cents more for Four Roses to get a lot better (than what?) whiskey. This was dramatized by showing a few shiny copper pennies in a glass of whiskey. The gimmick was acclaimed as a brilliant creative idea.

Soon people were heard complaining that Four Roses tasted "like copper pennies." Admen laughed this off. But sales drooped. Eventually the pennies were removed from the glasses. Then the price was cut. After that a new bottle was introduced. No one ever refers to the "clever copper pennies campaign" anymore.

Admen know that, above all, they must please the customer or might as well shovel the ad dollars down a sewer. Unfortunately they don't always follow this precept. They're usually too busy creating advertising and running a business to consider the consumer as an individual rather than in bulk as a "market." Working hard on a promotion, they tend to become blinded by personal enthusiasm. They see only the merits of the product, ads, promotion, from their own viewpoint. They don't see obvious faults that are so clear to you, the prospective customer—since you in turn are concerned only about your own self-interest, not the advertiser's.

Prof. John W. Crawford, chairman of the department of mass communications at Michigan State University, said: "Advertising alone will not create markets—it cannot accomplish much unless people really want the qualities of the product advertised. If people will not respond favorably to a product introduced in test markets *without* advertising, no amount of advertising will create a market for that product. No amount of advertising can force you to buy something you don't really want."

Think of your own reactions to advertising strictly as an individual. Realize that you meet an advertisement as though you're encountering a new acquaintance. The mere fact that the person speaks to you doesn't make you like him. The determining factor is whether or not you react favorably to what he says, how he says it, how he looks and acts as he talks to you.

The same is true of an advertisement. The fact that the advertising exists and confronts you—on TV, radio, print, or whatever—doesn't win your favor. The determining factor is what the advertising says to you, and how, and whether you're at all interested in the subject. It can arouse your antagonism as well as your approval and positive action. Many admen and advertisers, as well as critics who tend to inflate the impression of advertising's super-power, often forget this simple truth.

The concept that "advertising pays" is a fallacy. Advertising pays only if its effect on you is favorable. If not, the advertising dollars spent not only fail to win your approval and purchase—but act to sell you *off* the product, perhaps forever.

Those who claim you're a pushover don't know the hard facts of business life. Frustrated, bedeviled businessmen know better. A bulletin from a trade magazine, *Super Market Merchandising and the Discount Merchandiser*, warned advertisers accordingly:

> Grocery manufacturers and their advertising agencies need to "re-think" their marketing programs . . . it just isn't that easy any more to get a consumer franchise on a product, even for the biggest manufacturers. In the old days, most grocery manufacturers could get along on their brand reputation, adding a few items now and then at no great cost. Today, they need a multitude of products just to stay on the treadmill. The costs of marketing have become astronomical. According to A. C. Nielsen it takes $3 million worth of advertising to get about $10 million worth of sales during the first year of life of a new brand. What's more, the mortality rate on new products is enormous.

Advertising Age noted in a lead editorial how a heavily slanted appeal can backfire:

> The present battleground for the two detergents that are trying to convince housewives of their efficacy in both hot and cold water is Oklahoma City. And it would be nice to report that, though the clothes in the commercial are dirty, the copy approach is clean. But such is not the fact, it turns out, in the case of a test TV commercial for Colgate's Fab. . . . there is a scene shot in the Good Housekeeping Institute. In it a home economist spoons a raw egg mixture onto a cloth, lets it dry slightly, then cuts the material in two. One part is then washed

in cold water plus Fab, the other in hot water and Fab. Results: No trace of stain in either place, the commercial states.

But when the Good Housekeeping Institute was asked if it wasn't standard procedure to use cold water in removing protein stains like those made by raw eggs, the Good Housekeeping Institute people said yes, and added that hot water would only set the stain and make it harder to remove.

Most housewives know this. So when they watch this test for Fab . . . they simply chalk it up as another bit of unbelievable advertising.

. . . the battle to win the consumer is a long-range affair, and if she thinks she is being fooled she is quite capable of switching her "vote" from one coldwater detergent to another next time she enters the marketplace.

This instance was generously labeled "unbelievable advertising." You might describe it more harshly. This kind of suspect approach is one of the prime reasons for the public's marked suspicion of advertising in general, and for its failure to succeed in many specific campaigns.

Chapter

DOES ADVERTISING MANIPULATE YOU AT WILL?

24

"Everyone's opinion at best can only be a wild guess." That's the warning from an expert writing in an advertising trade magazine about the fallacy of predicting ad results. Because the public's reactions are neither malleable nor predictable, advertising failures abound. Usually they're swept under the rug to keep them out of sight and hopefully out of your mind. Here is just a sampling.

Even the biggest advertisers fall in the soup with a mighty splash, as is shown by this announcement: "Campbell Soup Company has informed food brokers that it is discontinuing its line of Red Kettle dry soup mixes after spending more than $10,000,000 to advertise them."

Shortly before, the president of another firm, Corn Products Company, told stockholders at the annual meeting that the company had "stubbed its toe" on Knorr Soups. It was switching to imports and giving up manufacture in the U.S. in spite of many millions expended in trying to force the soups down the American throat.

Probably the most shocking fiasco of advertising and business was the washout of the Edsel car produced by Ford. There was no limit to the amount of manufacturing, merchandising ability, research, and advertising power behind the Edsel. One of the biggest agencies—Foote, Cone and Belding—was appointed and went to work with supreme confidence and enthusiasm.

Years of effort and a fortune in money went into getting

everything as absolutely perfect as possible—design, motor, body. Every smallest detail in the ad campaign was studied, restudied, researched, and polished. Marketing strategy was worked out and reworked again and again to guard against error. The car was produced and "positioned" (a pet Madison Avenue term) for a favorite Madison Avenue target: "The younger executive or professional family on the way up."

Advertising campaigns were written, torn up, rewritten, rejected, approved, turned down again, and finally settled upon. The advertising agency modestly heralded the Edsel advertising, with the usual ad alley restraint, as "the greatest advertising campaign ever conceived."

Finally the Edsel was launched with furious fanfare, probably never equaled before in such a mass selling effort. The goal was set at 200,000 Edsel sales the first year. And then something totally unexpected happened. . . .

The cars didn't sell. By the end of two years, about 100,000 Edsels had been bought by the public, half the number that was tabbed for the *first* year's sales alone. A little more than two years after the first Edsel was introduced, the Ford Company announced that the Edsel operation was being discontinued. The loss was estimated generally to have been about $350 million.

Various explanations for the failure have been given. All the alibis can be boiled down to just five little words: *People did not like it.*

You, the public, didn't go for the name, design, motor, and hundreds of other things about the Edsel. You didn't give your reasons. You didn't have to. As with every other advertised or unadvertised product, all you had to do was say in effect, "I don't like it"—and walk away from it.

If a household product is not too costly, you may buy it once (but the Edsel was a major expenditure for a family). If you don't care much for the item, and the advertising keeps exhorting you, pleading for your purchase, you might even try a second time. But if it still doesn't please you, you're through with it, probably for all time. The "manipulators" can't manipulate you to buy it. The "persuaders" can't persuade you. No one knows that better or more sorrowfully than advertisers and their agencies.

Other notable failures among automobiles include the Cord, Duesenberg, Avanti, Packard, Velie, Overland, and Franklin. In other high-powered fields, heavily advertised Hit Parade, product of the American Tobacco Company, and dozens of other cigarette brands came in on a hurricane of costly ballyhoo and went out like a puff of smoke.

Speaking within the confines of the Detroit Adcraft Club, John Crichton, president of the American Association of Advertising Agencies, said: "The consumer is in the driver's seat. . . . [He is] both rational and irrational . . . shot full of foibles and idiosyncrasies, crotchety, hardboiled and given to inexplicable vagaries and whims . . . as far from a puppet as one can get."

Referring particularly to the mass of misrepresentations in theater ads, Ben Hecht observed: "The public is given to such paradoxes, and remains, somehow, unconfused by them." The fact that the advertiser fails to fool you is no excuse for the fraud in advertising. It should not dilute your condemnation of the deceptive approach based on the permissible lie. It does weaken belief in the veracity of *any* advertising.

Francis R. Elliott, president of the Borden Company, declared that "the statistics most frequently quoted for the survival rate of new food products is two out of ten." In spite of everything advertisers and their agencies can do, using vast sums, research, assorted merchandising and marketing tactics and promotions, cents-off coupons, free samples, two-for-one sales, overt and hidden persuasion, eight out of ten new products fail to win your favor.

How does this jibe with the claim of social critics that advertising can overpower the public? The fact is that people's heads contain brains, not Jell-O. No matter how much pressure is applied by the weight of ad dollars and absurd and deceptive appeals, you try a product and decide that you like it or not. No brand has public loyalty nailed down—ever.

Brand-switching is the name of the public's game that drives advertisers wild. It means that you bounce from purchase of one brand to another as you see fit. You buy soap A today, B with a special offer next week, and C with a two-for-one sale the week after. Yet each of the advertisers of brands A, B, and C is supposed to have you under his thumb.

If advertising pressure can force people to buy anything, why then are so many "special offers" made today as desperation measures pleading for you to buy the product? A count showed nearly fifty bargain entreaties in ads in just three national magazines in one month—excluding all other magazines, newspapers, TV, radio, etc.

The listing included many of the heaviest-spending advertisers imploring you:

"7¢ Off Coupon for New Lux Liquid."

"Free! Your First $2.00 Package of New Dawn Hair Color."

"25¢ Cash for Spaghetti with Borden's Parmesan Cheese."

It makes good sense to note the advertising and try a product once if it is useful and readily affordable. You're always looking for something better. Advertising advises you that it's offering that "something better" and urges you to try it. You do. If you like the product better than what you've been using, the advertising has succeeded in its excellent, productive function. The advertiser benefits. You and your family gain.

If not enough of the public like the item, if you turn thumbs down, the advertiser and his product are finished. Every ad dollar he spends in trying to sell you further only adds more to his loss.

This is true of the biggest as well as small advertisers. General Foods eyed the market for higher-priced "gourmet foods" and saw sales volume increasing rapidly. They noted that the successes in the field were principally small companies with miniscule resources compared to G.F. As the big company can afford to do, they invested extensive time and dollars in study and preparation.

General Foods could and did pay the highest-salaried recipe and food preparation experts, package designers, marketing planners, research brains, artists, writers, and the biggest agencies. The products in the slick new gourmet line were loudly touted as super in quality and taste. As expected, the items looked "like a million dollars." The prices were necessarily high. Sales were disappointingly low. Not enough families would pay so much for what they considered to be too little.

The mammoth company, its retinue of experts, and its giant agency tried other tactics, devised different campaigns, new marketing and advertising approaches. They poured in more and more money to make the gourmet line a success. Each new plan was presented with the enthusiastic exhortation that this would be the answer, the "open sesame" to overwhelm the public and produce big sales volume.

Nothing worked. After many costly battles, General Foods finally acknowledged that the war was lost. They killed the line and absorbed the profitless expenditure of millions of dollars.

In most every business, profits depend on repeat sales. However, there are some shifty entrepreneurs who turn out one inferior item after another, backing them with bombastic advertising, milking profits from the early sales surge—until people find out how unsatisfactory the product is. Then the crooks either unload the company on less canny businessmen or drop it. They go on to another inferior, fast-moving quickie that cheats the one-shot buyers.

The reputable advertisers, the so-called "supermen," rack up many losses which the public and stockholders never notice. These are the huge "hidden losses" suffered when management delays in producing items that the public is ready, willing, and eager to buy.

An example is the case of the low-calorie soft drinks. For years smaller local bottlers such as No-Cal and Cott were selling mounting quantities of low-calorie sodas. The big boys ignored the market, thinking it was a passing fancy. They underestimated the overriding desire of many people to be slim, more attractive, and healthier. In spite of the multimillion-dollar campaigns to buy more Coca-Cola, Pepsi-Cola,

Canada Dry, and other big sugar brands, sales soared for the smaller bottlers of low-calorie drinks. By sheer weight of advertising dollars they should have been crushed. Instead they flourished and grew.

Finally the giant advertisers introduced their own low-calorie brands, and found an enormous sales response. They immediately started bragging through their public-relations experts about their great successes. They didn't mention the multimillion-dollar "hidden losses" sustained by not offering the products earlier.

It took a comparatively small and little-known manufacturer, Wilkinson Blade Company of England, to introduce stainless steel blades notably in the U.S. Sales boomed remarkably. Gillette, Schick, and other "leaders" saw this, figured it as a flash in the pan. They marked time, finally gave in. Management didn't tell stockholders how many millions of dollars they lost by waiting so long to hop on the bandwagon of consumer desire.

All facets of the business combine to try to hush up any publicity that reveals the fallibility of "the infallible adman."

Chapter 25

SHOULD ADVERTISING BE ELIMINATED?

In the light of all the flaws and fraudulent aspects of advertising, should it be eliminated? Absolutely not. In spite of its evils, advertising embodies many indispensible benefits. There are lots of bright, able admen who are concerned about the public welfare as well as their own. But there is urgent need to change today's pervading immoral approach to advertising. Preferably this regeneration should be created by admen themselves.

It is most doubtful that such self-reform will be instituted and carried through adequately by the advertising industry. The many failures in the past have proved that self-regulation is almost impossible, as the few representative samples in this book have disclosed. There are hundreds more examples left untold because of space limitations.

In the spirit of self-regulation, the Association of National Advertisers and the American Association of Advertising Agencies jointly set up the Committee for the Improvement of Advertising Content. The purpose was to seek out complaints about ads. In two years, *only ten advertisements* were found to be in bad taste by the committee.

The auto companies knew for years that their cars had safety flaws, whether or not they were actually "unsafe at any speed." They had many warnings to adopt safety devices and regulations. After long delays in needed reforms, they still didn't take unified action. The government finally had to impose laws to *force* manufacturers to incorporate minimum safety features for every car.

Is there undue stress in this book on the reprehensible practices of advertising? Why not emphasize the honest ads? Because ads, like people, *should* be honest and truthful. When ads, like people, are dishonest, they must be criticized and exposed. That, unfortunately, covers a very large percentage of advertising.

Delivering the provost's lecture at Michigan State University, Prof. John W. Crawford said: "Advertising is an instrument in the hands of the people who use it. If evil men use advertising for base purposes, then evil can result. If honest men use advertising to sell an honest product with honest enthusiasm, then positive good for our kind of capitalistic society can result."

It was not until I was away from day-to-day advertising activity for over a year that I could look at Madison Avenue objectively. Then I realized (recognizing fully my own participation in such a course for decades) that the general approach of admen is based on *the permissible lie*.

Often without being specifically conscious of it, most admen tackle the selling of goods from the viewpoint of seeking to get away with whatever they can—*to the boundary of being punished legally*. The usual belief is that this course is necessary and therefore excusable.

Honest, interesting, informative advertising can be the most productive for the advertiser and agency over the long run. The benefits of advertising a good product can be enormous for all, as well as disastrous for an inferior product, as illustrated by a short short story:

Once there was a baker who baked very poor pies. Naturally he sold very few pies. He decided that he could sell more by advertising. So he placed an appealing ad in the local newspaper; he was a very able adman but an inferior baker.

Soon after he opened his shop the next morning, crowds of women attracted by the ad started pouring in for his pies.

His wife was delighted. But suddenly the baker yelled, "Lock the door! Don't let in any more customers!"

When the store had been emptied, he placed a sign on the door: "Sold out of pies." His wife complained, "But we still have dozens of unsold pies."

"I know," said the baker, "but I suddenly realized that if so many people find out how bad our pies are, they'll tell their friends. *Nobody* will ever come to our shop again. We'll be ruined. Before I advertise any more, I'll have to learn how to bake better pies."

That's just one of the important benefits of advertising: It tends to raise the quality of products offered for sale. Nothing fails faster than a poor product that has been boosted by heavy advertising.

For good or evil, advertising—as noted in a *Life* editorial —is a vital part of "the engine of the American economy." It's an essential activity of our economic system. Without advertising, our superior forms of manufacturing, marketing, and distribution which contribute to producing the highest average standard of living in the world could not exist.

The Gross National Product—which is the amount paid out annually in the U.S.A. for goods and services—is about $630 billion at this writing. That's about $112 billion gain in the past three years on record, and it's climbing (expected to be $1.2 trillion in 1975). Translated into terms of human consumption, about $90 billion is now spent just on food each year. The average big supermarket offers about 7,500 different food items. In a single market there is a choice of twenty-two kinds of baked beans.

Some critics of advertising and marketing contend that twenty-two different types and labels of baked beans are too many, creating waste. Is it really too wide a choice for the thousands of families shopping in a giant supermarket? Would 220 kinds of baked beans, or 2,200, be too many brands for almost 200 million people?

It has been said that "what critics call the wastefulness of advertising is really the price that has to be paid for freedom of choice." Furthermore there *is* plenty of choice between advertised and unadvertised labels, so the advertiser is not in the driver's seat.

Some social critics, although very much concerned about material gains and comforts for themselves, attack advertising indiscriminately, failing to realize and acknowledge that it is "the showcase of business"—controlled by business. Along with the evils, the benefits of both must be considered.

It is easy to forget that advertising functions on the smallest, most fundamental terms, as well as the largest. Not every ad is on costly TV programs or full color pages in print. This little sign tacked on a factory bulletin board is an ad for safety: "Girls, if your sweater is too large for you, look out for the machines. If you are too large for your sweater, look out for the machinists."

A simple letter can be a potent ad, such as this one: "Dear Mr. Walker. . . . In case you haven't noticed, we are busy painting at 19 Pine Lane, around the corner from you. We take great pride in our work, and want the finished job to reflect an attractive, well-kept neighborhood. While our men are at hand, we can offer you savings on a paint job that you may have planned for the near future. Why not drive over and see the work we do, then call us. Yours for a friendly handshake. . . . John Baraglia."

Mr. Walker was thinking about a paint job. He looked at Mr. Baraglia's work. He liked it. John's competitive bid won. Both of them gained through timely, honest, informative advertising.

It is fitting to have some leading practicing admen tell you of its benefits. "Art" (not Arthur) Tatham, board chairman of Tatham-Laird and Kudner agency, said: "Advertising plays one of the most important roles in providing people with the opportunity freely to that right [freedom of choice]. The exercise of choice depends on information. Advertising provides it . . . much of the task of good advertising is to portray as clearly and intimately as possible the way the product fits into the lives of the particular people it can best serve."

In a message addressed to "bright young men and women," the American Association of Advertising Agencies stated:

> The biggest objection to advertising seems to be that it makes people want things they *really don't need* . . . such things as refrigerator-freezers, air conditioners, movie cameras, sports cars, dishwashing machines, clothes dryers, frozen foods, instant foods, vitamins, new synthetic fibers for lightweight clothing, TV sets, stereo, hi-fi, *two* automobiles, more leisure time and the equipment to enjoy it: boats, skis, fishing and hunting equipment, fast travel by jet—just to name a few.
>
> Sure . . . we could get along without most of these "unnecessary" adjuncts to modern living—and we really wouldn't miss them if we turned back the clock to the days *before you were born.* For as you may or may not realize, most of these things came into real distribution *only during your young lifetime.* And *Advertising* helped make them all possible. So, in a broad sense . . . a *good part* of the *good life* you take for granted today has been stimulated by Advertising over the past twenty years. (The italics are the advertiser's.)

Challenged on this point of "unnecessary adjuncts," an adman was asked, "What in the world, for example, would a woman want with ten new dresses?" He answered quickly, "Ten new hats."

Lord Thomson, English newspaper magnate, wrote in *The Advertising Quarterly:* "Advertising is not expendable. It is not a garnishment of business, but an essential ingredient in our economy. . . . It makes jobs; it reduces selling costs; it helps increase our standard of living. Effectively and properly used, it increases productivity and makes possible the only security a company and its labor forces can hope to have in an uncertain world."

Again note the key phrase in the foregoing: Advertising "effectively and properly used." Most of the objections to advertising are on the score of prevailing *improper* usage.

Does advertising lower prices? The cost reduction process generally operates simply in this sequence:

1. Advertising informs you of the product and its availability.

2. If you try the product and like it, you buy more and tell others about it (unless offensive advertising then sells you off the product).

3. With increased sales, production goes up, cost per unit goes down. You get the benefit usually in lower prices.

Contrary to the belief of many, the more money spent on advertising by a company as sales increase, usually the lower the ad cost per unit. With autos, for example, according to Advertising Publications, Incorporated, the five top companies—American Motors, Chrysler, Ford, General Motors, and Studebaker—in one year increased their total advertising expenditures 5.6 percent. In the same year sales climbed 8.7 percent. Ad cost per car dropped 2.8 percent.

Several dozen people were asked how much of the average $3,000 they paid for their cars was advertising expense. Their guesses ranged from $200 to $500. They were influenced by the tremendous total advertising expenditures for cars—about $250 million in advertising in one year for the top five makers alone.

They were astonished to learn that the average advertising cost for the cars they bought was under $35. Chevrolet, which spent the most—about $65 million—sold over 2.1 million cars, with an ad cost of under $30 per car. On the other hand, Studebaker, which spent about $5.5 million sold about 65,000 cars—with an ad cost of about $85 each; this high cost was subsequently an ingredient in its downfall.

Advertisers keep trying to improve products. This is not due to a sense of public service but because each competitor is trying to outperform the other.

The non-advertiser can operate this way: He sells stores his X-label peas, usually by providing a price advantage and possibly (not necessarily) reducing quality. His product quality is more likely to vary since he has no large advertising investment in X-label to protect. He can profit until customers find X-label peas unsatisfactory. He then changes the name only, offering the same product as Y-label peas. He can continue under different labels, serving different stores.

The brand advertiser can't operate this way. If his quality

falters, the public stops buying it. His brand dies, and perhaps his business with it.

The retailer in some instances displays and pushes the private label (unadvertised) product because he may make an eight-cent profit on the twenty-five-cent package, compared with a five-cent profit on the advertised brand. Other retailers give best display to the advertised brand because they found that they sell ten packages at a five-cent profit for a total fifty-cent profit. In the same period of time, they sell five packages of the unadvertised label at eight-cents profit each—a total forty-cent profit—ten cents less total profit than on the advertised brand.

How much profit per package the retailer makes doesn't concern you, of course. You choose—you decide. It's so simple: You buy a can of Del Monte peaches for fifty-three cents. You see unadvertised Delbel peaches for forty-nine cents for the same size can. You try both. If you find Delbel as good as Del Monte, you'll keep buying it and saving four cents per can. Not $1 billion spent on advertising could force you to buy Del Monte against your wishes.

The advertised brand has the advantage of familiarity. Henry Slesar, head of Slesar and Kanzer agency, wrote a famous ad for McGraw-Hill magazines. It showed a stony-faced man staring coldly out at the reader. He was saying: "I don't know who you are. I don't know your company. I don't know your company's product. I don't know your company's reputation. Now—what is it you wanted to sell me?"

Advertising makes it easier for you to *sample* a product and decide for yourself. The largest single order to date in the history of the Cedar Rapids, Iowa, post office was from Quaker Oats cereal mill. It consisted of thirty-five boxcars of 5.7 million sample boxes of Cap'n Crunch pre-sweetened corn and oats cereal. The postage alone cost Quaker Oats about $180,000. People liked the samples and bought the big boxes in stores, scoring a quicker success for Quaker.

Many of the big advertised brands—Daffodil Farm Bread, Vicks Formula 44, Baggies, Yuban Instant Coffee, Kraft dressings, and thousands more—owe some of their success to free or cut-price sampling. Is this any way to run a business, spending a half million dollars and more in one shot to give away your advertised product *free*?

You bet it is—if the product is good.

But—like the baker's pies—if the product is bad, each ad dollar added will kill it quicker.

Chapter 26

ADMEN AS INDIVIDUALS—AND COLLECTIVELY

I have encountered a higher percentage of phonies on Madison Avenue than in any other walk of business life. I also know many advertising people who are hard-working, intelligent, extremely able, and decent. The latter will applaud secretly, if not openly, the revelations here about advertising's faults and the vital need for correction.

Any rating of admen, as with any other grouping, must consider the individual. Listings in newspapers and magazines reveal a high percentage of admen among leaders promoting the public welfare. Although such activity is sometimes tabbed "good business," I believe that the reason is overwhelmingly a desire on the part of those progressive individuals to contribute and serve others. The advertising press abounds with items such as these:

"Lawrence W. Howe, partner of Gerson, Howe & Johnson, has been elected a director of United Cerebral Palsy of Greater Chicago."

"Among those working for Letchworth Village school for retarded children are Herb Silverman, *Glamour;* Alan Yablon, Doyle Dane Bernbach; Joe Hanley, WCBS; Don Foote, Young & Rubicam; Delight Dixon, Warner Bros. Co."

"Oscar Lubow, vp Young & Rubicam, appointed to Adult Education Committee."

"Elmo Ellis, WSB, Atlanta, elected a director of the Georgia Arthritis & Rheumatism Foundation."

"Charles H. Brower, chairman, BBDO, will serve as national chairman of the United Community Campaigns of America."

"Taking posts in the Community Service Society are John Elliott, Jr., senior vp of Ogilvy, Benson & Mather; Edward Kroepke, assistant ad manager, *New York Daily News;* Bayard E. Sawyer, publisher of *Business Week.*"

"Austin Thomas, vp of Benton & Bowles, heads a committee for the United Hospital Fund."

Responsibility in business life is another matter. King Edward VIII, better known as the Duke of Windsor, abdicated because "the heavy burden of responsibility" was impossible to carry under the circumstances. Many admen say the same in private about having any special accountability to the public in preparing and carrying through advertising. They say flatly that their specific and sole loyalty is to their clients, to help them make a profit.

I disagree. I believe that advertising is in a special category in its responsibility to the public and to the nation. Advertising, as is loudly acclaimed by its leaders, is the bridge between business and the public. Yet, while serving as a link, too many admen feel responsibility only to increase business profits, with little or no regard for the public welfare. They assume no accountability to convey the truth to the public.

The Advertising Council runs "public-service advertising" expressed as "Uncommon Advertising for the Common Good." It cites campaigns for U. S. Savings Bonds, Peace Corps, United Nations, Radio Free Europe, American Red Cross, Forest Fires Prevention, Keep America Beautiful (no comment on billboard advertising), United Community Campaigns, U.S.A.—and other worthy causes. It states that this "power for good is something new and hopeful in the world."

With all its fine purpose, much of the Advertising Council material strikes me as uncommonly mild, even weak. Agencies contribute a good deal of time and effort—but usually far from their best thinking and abilities. The council acts in effect somewhat as a token handout, a way of alibiing when criticized, "Look, here's what Madison Avenue is doing for the public and the nation. Now leave us alone, stop heckling."

There are a few notable exceptions in public-service campaigns into which admen put hard work, dedication, and even their own money contributions. This usually happens when the principals are fighting for a cause they're enthusiastic about as individuals.

Agency heads Carl Ally and William Bernbach battled competitively on the agency front. As individuals they cooperated on behalf of the Clean Air movement to combat air pollution in New York City. The result was a campaign of effective information ads like one headlined: "TOMORROW MORNING WHEN YOU GET UP, TAKE A NICE DEEP BREATH. IT'LL MAKE YOU FEEL ROTTEN."

Delighted by the efforts, Mrs. Carter F. Henderson, vice president of the citizen's organization, said: "My faith in the advertising business has been restored. All our little group could do was sit back and watch the powers of business at work."

Many admen have a sense of humor about their self-acknowledged foibles. Batten, Barton, Durstine and Osborn (usually called Beebee, Dee and Oh on Madison Avenue) kidded its own name in an agency presentation listing other possible agency name combinations including: Fine Kettle Fish, Incorporated; Thrust, Parry and Lunge; Butcher, Cleaver and Block, Incorporated; Shad, Rowe and Bacon.

There is no question that admen and advertising can perform advantageously for the public. Yet the factual evidence is dominant that Madison Avenue operates with the primary aim not to serve the public but to *have the public serve advertising and business.* A few glimmers of kindly light through the dense fog of permissible lying does little to relieve the moral darkness deepened by *bad*vertising's perverting influence.

Until the advertising field actually functions with a much greater, predominating sense of social responsibility—not just claims to do so—it will remain suspect.

Chapter 27

MUST ADS LIE TO SUCCEED?

The two most effective ads I've ever heard about were real "life-savers":

The First State Bank of Morton, Texas, ran a full-page ad in the Morton *Tribune* during a long drought that threatened to kill local crops. The ad read: "WANTED . . . Any Time —In The Next Two Weeks . . . *ANY OLD KIND OF TWO-INCH* RAIN . . . Apply With Little Thunder and Lightning . . . ALL OVER THE MORTON TRADE AREA." The ad worked—the two-inch rain came through in the time specified.

The other ad, even more powerful, was described by Mark Twain. He told about a man in Hannibal, Missouri, who used to sit in front of the village hotel daily reading his newspaper. One day he noticed a small patent medicine ad which read: "Cut this out. It may save your life." He cut out the ad. Continuing his reading, he looked through the hole and saw an enemy sneaking up on him with a knife. He dropped the paper, grabbed a chair, and knocked out the attacker. There was an ad, Twain concluded, that really saved a man's life.

Even admen who are ready to promise most any miracle rarely boast of such power in their ads. Yet, too often, as you know well, they concoct what turns out to be, consciously or not, irritation and deception. Writing effective advertising in my experience can be as simple as talking to the other person forthrightly—all too rare on Madison Avenue.

One night I was working late over the typewriter in the

agency offices. A mailroom boy hovered uncertainly outside my door. I called out, "You want me?"

He walked into my office slowly, stopped, shifted uneasily. A tall, skinny, pleasant-faced young man with that eager-beaver look.

I smiled tiredly. "Anything I can do for you?"

"I'd like to learn how to write ads."

"Ever try to write any?"

"No."

"How do you know you can write?"

"I'm sure I can."

I repressed a sigh. "Well, look over some of the ads of the accounts here and write some new ones. Then show them to me."

He thanked me, then hesitated. "I don't quite know how to start. I guess I have to write a lot of clever and fancy words like in most ads I see, some razzle-dazzle to fool the public. And I suppose I've gotta keep those five points in mind—"

"What five points?"

He seemed baffled by my stupidity. "You know, five points—I read them somewhere: arresting the interest, focusing the attention, and—"

"Don't worry about any five points, or being clever or fancy. Just pick a product to sell and then tell people in your copy how it will benefit them."

"But I wouldn't know where to start. I need something tricky, some screwball gimmick to get attention, don't I?"

I winced. "No. It's this easy: Pretend you're behind a retail store counter. A customer is in front of the counter. Now, what you'd say to sell him in person is what you write to sell him through an ad. You talk to him about what interests *him* about the product. Get it?"

"Hmmm. What should I say to him to get rolling?"

I tried another approach. "You ever sell anything to anyone?"

"Sure. I sold storm windows before going back to college during one vacation."

"Fine. What did you do? Did you put on a clown's makeup before you rang the doorbell? Or stand on your head to get attention? Or spout some insulting nonsense or deception at them? Or tell your prospects about those five points of salesmanship?"

"Gee, no. I said something like, 'You can cut your heating cost 20 percent next winter.'"

"There's your headline. Go on from there to write your ad."

"Gosh," he grinned, "writing advertising is easy."

He left, very chipper.

I turned back to the typewriter and pecked out: "You can cut your heating costs 20 percent next winter." The only trouble was that I was writing an ad about brassiéres.

Faking and fooling the public is *not* essential. "Truth in advertising" paid off for Ira A. Hirschmann, who inspired exceptionally successful advertising at Bamberger's, Lord and Taylor, Saks Fifth Avenue, and Bloomingdale's. He asserts that producing effective advertising is simple but that too often admen make it complicated and phony.

As a sparky youngster, he sought a job in the ad department of a leading store. He was challenged by the adman eager to write an ad to sell a batch of immovable green neck ties. A collection of beautiful neckties at $7 each had been a sellout—except for 207 green neckties. They'd tried every ad gimmick, even cutting the price to $2, but nothing worked. Apparently men just didn't like green.

Ira asked, "Did you try telling the truth?" Guffaws. He left.

He wrote an ad headlined: "OUR BUYER MADE A BAD MISTAKE!" The copy told what had happened and concluded: "If there are 207 men who like a green tie, they can get these magnificent $7 imported specimens for $5—because very few men like green neckties."

The ties sold out fast. As Oliver Wendell Holmes said: "You needn't fear to handle the truth roughly; she is no invalid."

Volkswagen and Doyle Dane Bernbach racked up one of advertising's biggest successes with mostly simple, straightforward ads. Sales went from two cars the first year to some 400,000 in fifteen years. The advertising told the facts of economy, durability, and dependability. They did not boast of beauty. A typical headline asked candidly: "DO YOU THINK THE VOLKSWAGEN IS HOMELY?"

When you ask admen what should be in a good ad, they often say something like what Mrs. Gladys H. Stoll, president of The Pure Food Company, stated in an advertising magazine: "The food industry is responsible for some of the best and some of the worst advertising. . . . I believe good food ads should be written from the woman's point of view. They should be helpful, informative and knowledgeable . . . exciting, compelling, attention-getting."

Strangely, something happens between what a good ad "should be" and is (this include's some of Pure Food's ads which, in my opinion, don't meet the excellent specifications). Admen tend to fool themselves about their product's virtues so that they go way overboard. This story was told by Roger M. Blough, chairman of the board of U. S. Steel:

"Two cows were standing by the pasture fence bordering the highway, when one of those big stainless-steel tank-trucks came along. Lettered on the side of the truck were the words: 'Superior milk . . . Pasteurized . . . Homogenized . . . Irradiated . . . Enriched with Vitamin D.' One cow turned to the other and said: 'Makes you feel kind of inadequate, doesn't it?' "

Do successful "good" ads have to be dull, as admen often insist? Not at all. The straightforward and highly effective campaigns cited previously refute that trite Madison Avenue lazyman's alibi.

A notable problem is that most national advertisers usually can't tell whether a theme is working effectively for some length of time, or ever, since there is no quick, precisely traceable response as with coupon orders. Too many factors influence sales results—including distribution, amount of store display, and local competitive problems, not just the advertising.

There is also a long lag between the time advertisers start putting products into stores, especially new items or "improved" versions, and when they know whether or not you're taking them off store shelves. The process is known as "filling the pipelines." Much silly, ineffectual advertising gets by for months, even a year or more, before the sales curve shows significant slumping. Even with good sales, the advertiser never knows whether the success couldn't have been greater with better advertising.

Must ads rely on tricks? Gimmicks? Clever word-twists? Fakery? No. An increasing success for decades is Dr. Scholl's Foot Products. The ads have laid it on the line, year after year: "FEET HURT? CUT YOUR OWN CUSHIONING FOOT PLASTER FOR FAST RELIEF." "STOPS CORN PAIN ALMOST INSTANTLY—SUPER-SOFT ZINO-PADS." Dr. Scholl's progress was always based on reminding people straight-out of their problems, and offering solutions that work.

An effective food ad was headlined simply: "$1.00 DISH—MAKES 4 SERVINGS—MADE WITH CAMPBELL'S SOUPS." The bubbling color photo showed a tempting "Frankfurter Crown Casserole—Almost a meal-in-one-dish for less than one dollar." Complete with recipe. No hi-jinks. No fakery. It sold a lot of Campbell's Cream of Mushroom Soup.

Metropolitan Life Insurance Company has rendered excellent service and sold billions of dollars worth of policies with their specifically helpful health ads. Their ad that tells what to do about possible symptoms of cancer, in one instance, has actually saved lives, according to doctors whose patients came in for a check-up after reading the ad. And the public-serving ads have helped Metropolitan to healthy, profitable business.

Unknowing critics have pointed to the famous Ogilvy "black eye patch ad" for Hathaway Shirts, saying: "Here's proof that all you have to do is toss an absurd gimmick into an ad, shove enough dollars behind it, and you've got the lame-brained public buying."

It's true that the ad helped lift Hathaway sales from under $5 million a year to over $12 million. But the eye patch was significant primarily because it caught attention, as a departure from the usual flawlessly handsome, phony-looking models habitually used before. The superb photo also revealed the shirt fabric quality so clearly that it practically placed a sample in the reader's hands.

Most important, the copy told in detail how the Hathaway shirt differed from the "ordinary, mass-produced shirt . . . tailored more *generously,* and is therefore more *comfortable.* The tails are longer, and stay in your trousers . . . remarkable *fabrics* collected from the four corners of the earth —Viyella and Aertex from England, woolen taffeta from Scotland, Sea Island cotton from the West Indies, handwoven madras from India, broadcloth from Manchester, linen batiste from Paris, hand-blocked silks from England, exclusive cottons from the best weavers in America."

That detailed, convincing information made the sale. If it were the eye patch alone, then the horde of Madison Avenue imitators would have succeeded instead of failing with their tasteless devices—red-painted shoes, screwball hats, Indian chief haircuts. They all failed because you don't buy nonsensical gimmicks, you go for benefits for yourself.

Virginia Miles of Young and Rubicam told the Grocery Manufacturers of America in respect to gimmickry: "Attention is not the whole story. Otherwise the most successful ad would be, I suppose, a picture of a naked lady in a bathtub, preferably standing up."

That the public wants and seeks informative advertising is proved by the enormous growth in the past decade of weekly "shopping newspapers" which contain little more than detailed informative ads. Some include a sprinkling of local names and news. Families read the ads which fill from 75 percent to all the pages—and they buy. Otherwise advertisers wouldn't stay in. Their ads are "news" to the housewife particularly, as are supermarket and other retail ads in the daily newspapers.

Retail store ads are more likely to be down to earth, giving the facts, details, and prices people want—as many ads for national brands don't. There are three primary reasons for this difference:

1. Most store ads can be checked for sales results in a day to a week. This tends to eliminate frippery that doesn't sell goods.

2. Department heads squawk fast about copy they don't understand, which they realize would be meaningless to you too. Deceptive claims are apt to result in merchandise returned in a hurry by angry customers.

3. Most store ads are turned out under great pressure involving high speed in preparation. There just isn't time to toss in the usual self-indulgent Madison Avenue monkeyshines.

It's a strange phenomenon, however, that when department stores use TV, their commercials customarily blast and bray in imitation of the usual raucous and offensive pattern. Perhaps that's why so many department store admen say, "Somehow, TV advertising doesn't work for us."

The American Association of Advertising Agencies spent a lot of money for a study to determine what consumers say they want and don't want in ads. They concluded that people want ads with specific information, details, and prices, ads that are useful and identify the reader with the product or service. Further, people don't want ads that are unrealistic, that make the individual feel he's being treated as foolish, moronic, or gullible, nor ads that are repetitious, boring, or irritating.

Are these answers any surprise to you? No. Will most advertisers and agencies learn and follow these expensive "findings"? Not a chance.

In my experience, most admen will, as always, give pious, approving lip service to "informative, useful, public-serving advertising." Primarily they will proceed as always, creating "madvertising" to get an okay from Mr. Big—while trying to please themselves and impress each other as much as they possibly can.

Chapter

HOW TO IMPROVE WHAT YOU DON'T LIKE

28

Edmund Burke wrote in the 1700's: "All that is necessary for the triumph of evil is that good men do nothing."

The point is more pertinent today in respect to evils touched on here in advertising and business—as well as in politics, social conduct, and other aspects of daily living. If there is anything you don't like about advertising and TV, for example, and you sit back and do nothing about it, then you may deserve whatever fraud or irritation or other noxious emanation is inflicted on you.

"What can I do?" asked a lady who had been griping against TV commercials. Here are the answers:

Stop buying the product that's advertised in those commercials.

Stop buying every product made by that advertiser.

Above all, write to the advertiser that you're putting *all* his products on your "don't buy" list and that you're urging friends to do the same. Address your letter to the *president* of the company, nobody else.

Don't just gripe about it, act. Write your complaint also to the president of your local station and to the network.

The above rules apply to better TV and radio programming too—demand specific improvement, tell exactly how and why. Taking over the job as chairman of the Federal Communications Commission, Rosel H. Hyde emphasized that television has a responsibility to *inspire* as well as to entertain and inform. Your letters will help to inspire and bring about improved programming.

A significant letter and answer appeared in a syndicated newspaper column:

"Dear Ann Landers. . . . the current crop of TV shows is enough to make a person sick . . . here is what we are getting in Grand Rapids, Mich.: At noon, 'Love of Life'—a school girl is expecting a baby. At 3:00 P.M., 'General Hospital,' a school girl is expecting a baby. At 4:00 P.M., 'Secret Storm,' a school girl is expecting a baby. After supper we get 'Peyton Place'—and another school girl expecting a baby. Comment, please. Mrs. E.M."

"Dear Mrs. M.: Complain—to the sponsor."

It's so easy to complain—and then reach for another brand on the store shelf. Exercise your freedom of choice. Every time you pass up the offending brand on the shelf, you're registering another protest. If enough people boycott the brand (along with writing a letter), the offensive TV advertising and programs will diminish.

Your actions can and will bring on improvement. Write to the presidents at the networks; you don't need their personal names—write "President, NBC, CBS, or ABC, New York City." Also write to local stations and sponsors (always to the president), advising that a carbon or copy is going to the FCC. Write to your Congressmen and Senators. Write to Chairman, Federal Communications Commission, Washington, D.C.

Former FCC chairman E. William Henry said that he saw no necessity for government-subsidized networks, new legislation, or other "magic remedies" to raise TV standards; rather, improvement is up to each individual: "If you don't like the kind of program your local TV station is offering, write to them and tell them. If you don't get any cooperation from the station, write to the FCC and tell us about it. A station's broadcasting license comes up for renewal every three years, and any complaint about its service that is not obviously frivolous goes into the file for consideration at renewal time."

You have this powerful weapon: Right now TV and radio station licenses are renewed almost automatically. As mentioned, no TV license has yet been revoked, to my knowledge. In fact, stations are trying to get the three-year renewal period lengthened to five years.

A mass of letters to the FCC criticizing specific programs, commercials, or over-commercialization on a local station will hold up automatic license renewal. The least that will happen to the station is a very troublesome and frightening FCC investigation—far worse than a visit from the income tax man. The result could be loss of a broadcasting license worth millions of dollars.

With enough public protest, there will be a first TV license revocation, and many more where justified. This hits the broadcaster in the only place where it really matters to him—his pocketbook.

What Herbert Hoover said way back in 1922 as Secretary of Commerce still applies: "Radio [true also now of TV] is not to be considered merely as a business carried on for private gain, for private advertisement, or for the entertainment of the curious. It is to be considered primarily from the standpoint of public interest."

Station owners and advertisers don't agree. Their actions prove that their overriding concern is private profit. The government has been acquiescent. Sixty million families can raise an angry din that will change this—*if you will.*

A promising united effort is growing. In some communities, groups of women are getting together about once a week for productive letter-writing sessions. They enjoy a discussion about TV programs and commercials, national and local political developments, school issues, and other timely topics. Then each takes pen in hand and writes one or more letters on the spot—complaining, complimenting, seeking action. They address presidents of companies, networks, representatives, right up to the President of the United States. Perhaps you'd care to start such a discussion-and-action group.

It's effective to send applause as well as gripes. If you enjoy a program particularly, find the commercials bearable, and wish to reward the sponsor by purchasing his product, write and tell him so. Such letters are warmly acknowledged. They can't help but elevate standards of TV programming and commercials. Every president prefers to be thought of as a "good guy," especially when your letters show him it's good business.

We wrote to the local phone company head: "Our entire family must compliment you and thank you most warmly for your wisdom in forming your policy of not breaking commercials into your wonderful evening programs and Young People's Concerts. . . . Your commercials have worked with us, causing us to have our four phones switched to the push-button type. You are creating a splendid image for your company." (*The New York Times* stated: "By clearly dividing TV's editorial and commercial content, A.T.&T. is the year's pace-setter in progressive television behavior.")

C. W. Owens, president of the New York Telephone Company, replied: "I am delighted you enjoy our programs. Your comments on the placement and quality of our commercials was especially nice to hear. . . . From all the letters and critical acclaim we received, we are sure that TV viewers agree with your sentiments. . . . Your words made a big hit with me!"

TV columnist Jack O'Brien stressed the power of letters in an article in *Cosmopolitan:*

> Networks, sponsors, advertising men, stars, somehow do take note of their mail. The most cynical, most coldly pragmatic program man . . . must also know that a rising assault of mail indicates that he will only hurt his own chances if he hews to his position.
>
> But *someone* has to bring the wrong to the attention of someone or, like the tree falling in the forest which has no one within hearing distance and consequently makes no noise, the fiercely convinced letter you never write, the intelligent conviction you never voice, can be of no avail.

I assure you from the *inside* of Madison Avenue that the right critical letter to the president of the company gets plenty of attention. Typically, one day I received a hurried phone call from the client's admanager: "Drop everything! The boss called one of his emergency meetings. Hurry over!"

We took our seats apprehensively at the conference table. Had someone at the agency made some terrible error? Were we about to get the axe? Others were just as disturbed; one could almost hear the ulcers perforating.

The president entered, his frown ominous. He whipped a letter from his pocket and started reading, his voice trembling with anger: "Dear Mr. President. . . ." The letter was from a housewife. She complained about last week's TV program, rapping the "irritating and insulting commercials."

The head man stared coldly. "This woman writes me, 'Your products are excellent. If your advertising was a fraction as good, we'd keep buying them. But we can't stand looking at your TV commercials which address our entire family as idiots. Until the tone of your advertising changes, we're not buying *anything* your company makes. Our friends and neighbors feel the same way.' "

He spat a curse, resumed reading. " 'I've told the manager of our local Safeway supermarket where I shop that we're boycotting your products. He has seen your commercials and agrees with us. We regret this action because you know how to make fine quality products, as well as terrible commercials.' "

The president put down the letter, his face richly purpled. He said in a choked voice, "I've had other letters like that from *my* customers. This one does it. I want those goddamned lousy commercials off the air as of now! I want to see some new storyboards that make sense and don't insult the intelligent people who buy *my* products. I want to see new ideas in three days or else. . . ."

The admanager said carefully, "But those commercials rated very high in the Schwerin tests. Sales have been going good—"

The head man interrupted, "Our products are so good that they sell in spite of putrid, insulting advertising. I've let all you *bright* boys talk me into using those ridiculous commercials even though I disliked them personally. But now I'll say it—*my wife hates them too!* And I'll tell you wise guys something else—" He waved the letter like a flag. "*My wife is a housewife too!* She's just like this average housewife who had the kindness to tell me why we've lost her as a customer. My friends at the club hate our commercials. They're constantly ribbing me about them. And they're consumers too! If you fellows can't come up with some effective commercials that treat our customers as intelligent human beings, then I'll get an agency that can. That's final!"

Not every letter has that effect. But each sensible, factual, forthright letter hits the mark—when addressed to the president. Don't write to the complaint department, or the advertising manager, or the advertising agency. They're inclined to suppress such letters by saying, "Just another crackpot." After all, each complaint is a criticism of their work.

Usually the president cares. That's one of the factors which made him president. He may not call a meeting. He may simply scrawl across the top of your letter: "Action! Send me carbon of your reply. E. J. R." The man he sends it to for "action!" jumps to it generally. If you don't get an answer, write to the president again. Tell him you wrote before—include a carbon of your previous letter, if available. State that you received no reply and are waiting to tell more friends and retailers about the discourtesy. You'll get "action"!

Don't write a nasty, cussing letter. Such missives go deservedly into the "screwball" file. State your gripe and facts briefly and clearly. As "consumers," our family has written quite a few complaint letters. We've always received a reply, usually a satisfactory and effective one.

We wrote this letter to the president of Procter and Gamble:

Kindly be advised that after using Crest for a year, with complete satisfaction, we have now switched to another brand of toothpaste as a protest against your repetitive commercials since we find them so irritating. We've heard many of our friends complain against the Crest TV commercials to the point of revolting against the product, but they don't bother to tell you so. We believe you have a right to know our viewpoint. No more of *any* Procter & Gamble products for us as long as the offensive commercials continue.

Within a week a long letter arrived from a Procter and Gamble executive expressing thanks and regrets: "I want you to know that I am sharing your letter with our advertising people directly in charge of Crest so that they will be aware of your reaction to the commercials." He advised that new commercials were in preparation: "We hope . . . they will meet with your approval . . . and we hope you will decide to continue using Crest."

Not just because of that one letter, but because there must have been many complaints, Crest commercials changed. They eliminated the hysterical kids screaming unbelievingly about "winnin' de toot'pase test." We're back to Crest, even though their new commercials will never win the Peabody Award. We thanked Procter and Gamble accordingly.

Start your personal crusade. Don't let advertisers get away with anything, even little things. Here's an incident that's trifling but an example of how to complain effectively. A neighbor bought some ice cream at A & P which was unsatisfactory. She shrugged it off, "I'll never buy their ice cream again."

We advised, "Don't take it lying down like most others do. That's why advertisers get away with so much. Usually the top man doesn't even know what's going on. Do something about it."

She wrote to the head of A & P: "You'll wish to know that we've just gone through our second half-gallon box of your Marvel Vanilla Fudge Ice Cream which consisted of about 99½ percent vanilla and ½ percent fudge. Since the contents are nothing like the tempting fudge-and-vanilla photo printed on the outside of the box, does this constitute fraudulent advertising? We wanted you to know that we're very much surprised at this misrepresentation by A & P, and we'll never buy your ice cream again."

As usually happens in such cases, the ceiling blew off. A

letter came from A & P: "We sincerely appreciate your interest . . . we are glad you let us know instead of remaining quietly dissatisfied. . . . We are looking into your complaint, contacting the packer involved. Thank you again for bringing the matter to our attention."

A letter arrived from the manager of Sealtest Foods division of National Dairy Products: "We are the manufacturers of Marvel Ice Cream. I have just received a phone call from the offices of A & P stating your dissatisfaction. Thank you for taking the time to write. . . . The quality of our products and the condition in which you received them are of the utmost importance to us. . . ." He advised that they were checking possible "disarrangement in our manufacturing process." He included a coupon good for two free half-gallons. The letter concluded: "I am sure that you will find our products satisfactory and to your liking."

The coupons bought some vanilla fudge ice cream loaded with chocolate like the picture on the box. Whether or not the letter was responsible, some correction was made in the manufacturing. The complaint helped A & P, Sealtest, and all who buy Marvel Ice Cream.

It is said that "Bad officials are elected by good citizens who don't vote." Similarly, faulty products and fraudulent, offensive advertising exist primarily because of good citizens who don't protest.

The Richmond, Indiana *Palladium-Item* reported: "How often we hear someone say he has no intention of voting because his vote won't count anyway. . . . In 1960 the Presidency was decided by 112,803 votes. Since there were 166,256 precincts, an increase amounting to one voter per precinct could have changed the result."

Your letters of complaint, which are your "votes," carry even more weight than your political vote. That's because advertisers know that overwhelming numbers of people are too lazy to write. They're aware that your one letter of complaint may well represent many families who feel the same way but don't write. Thus your one little letter packs a wallop delivered by masses of families. Send your complaints *now*. Keep writing your honest, factual gripes. Play fair. When the advertiser answers your complaint and does what you want about it, write your thanks.

The advertiser understands the value of your good will and patronage, and honors you accordingly. The non-advertiser figures he has little to lose, so he often ignores complaints unless you state that you're sending a copy to the store where you bought his product. Then you generally get action, since he doesn't want to lose the store as his customer.

In the case of something you bought at a store, write to the store president if you don't get satisfaction in a personal call at the store. Send a carbon to the manufacturer of the product. Hit them *both* for best results.

The reputable mail order advertiser is particularly anxious to satisfy because he wants you to buy again and again. With most, the business would fail if only one sale were made per customer. An opening page of a large mail order catalog featured a personal message from the president: "I offer my assurance of satisfaction. If you have ever been disappointed with anything you ever bought here at any time, please write to me personally and I will do my best to see that you are completely satisfied. Our success is built on your satisfaction."

The key sentence is what most every advertiser knows: "*Our success is built on your satisfaction.*" They mean it. Make your dissatisfactions known. Silence here is not golden, neither for you nor the advertiser.

If you're not satisfied—after registering a complaint—with anything received through the mail, the post office provides an extra recourse. Some literature in the mail offered catalogs of "top-brand merchandise at wholesale discounts." To receive the catalogs and become a "buying member," we sent three dollars for which we'd receive three "$1.00 merchandise certificates." Thus the three dollars would be returned on our first order. The seller also guaranteed money back if not satisfied.

The catalogs we received were appalling, and we wrote for

our money back: "Your listings are primarily of 'junk.' Your prices are higher than comparable nationally advertised brands at reputable discount stores." We waited. No reply. No money back.

We wrote again that if the refund didn't arrive in five days, carbons of the complaint letter would go to the local postmaster and to Washington. The money came by return mail. Try that—it works. The Post Office Department suggests: "If you feel that you are the victim of mail fraud . . . write, telephone or telegraph to your nearest Postal Inspector, or to: Chief Postal Inspector, U. S. Post Office Dept., Washington, D.C. 20260."

Chapter

HOW TO GET FULL VALUE ON YOUR PURCHASES

29

Your best protection in avoiding fraud in product quality is to select carefully from advertised brands and to deal with established stores. They honor your complaints and make refunds, protecting their advertising investments. They depend on your repeat purchases for their continuing sales and profits, and know that a store's best advertisement is a satisfied customer.

Some advertising, such as window signs in a fly-by-night store, may be outright fraud. Here are some tips on protecting yourself in such situations and others, avoiding losses, and getting just recompense:

Demand satisfaction immediately. Don't put it off. Return the merchandise and get a refund if you're disappointed. It's your right to seek and get your money's worth, to make the advertiser and seller live up to every claim and promise.

Always get and keep store sales slips, marking name, date, and item on them if not clear. Insist on getting such receipts, just as most stores reasonably insist on seeing your proof of purchase to show that you didn't buy the item elsewhere.

If you don't get satisfaction, tell the seller that you'll write to your local District Attorney, or to the Attorney General, the Bureau of Consumer Fraud, or your state government. If it becomes necessary, do so. Many states have a bureau of consumer fraud. If yours does not, your state Attorney General has the power and will to act in your behalf.

You may also write or call your local Better Business Bureau. Its power, however, is limited. The Better Business Bureau is supported by reputable businesses. It works hard to persuade violators to conform by voluntary self-regulation. Other than its own pressures, it has no enforcement power. Out-and-out crooks pay little attention to requests which carry no ability to punish.

Your Bureau of Consumer Fraud, Attorney General, and District Attorney have state and local enforcement power. Their intervention can lead to fine and imprisonment for anyone defrauding you. Your recourse to these authorities means something to violators.

Beware of misrepresentation by companies with questionable names, as on debt collector forms. The FTC stopped the Intrastate Credit Control Systems from using the name "State Bureau of Credit Control." Intrastate sold and remailed forms like this: "We MUST hear from you within ten days or this account will be turned over to—State Bureau of Credit Control." Other forms bearing a return address in state capital cities had the signature of "Alfred L. Burr" over the title "State Collection Supervisor," along with the statement, "Referred to file of County Collection Supervisor." The printed sheets had no official backing whatsoever.

If you find that a food, drug, or cosmetic you buy is mislabeled, unsanitary, or otherwise suspect in any way—and you can't get satisfaction from the store and/or maker—complain to the Bureau of Regulatory Compliance, Food and Drug Administration (FDA), U. S. Department of Health, Education and Welfare, Washington, D.C. 20204. Or write to the FDA in the major city nearest you (see the telephone directory under "U. S. Government"). Include in your report the product label and code number or any other special identifying markings, along with the name and address of the store where you bought the item. Send a carbon to the store president.

Be wary of stores that advertise close-outs and such suspect sales, especially when you are in a strange city. Look for the city license sales certificate in the store window as an official close-out.

Beware of offers of wholesale prices on retail goods. There's often some deceptive reason if a price seems too low. If unbelievable bargains are offered or advertised, it's safer not to believe them. This does not apply to nationally advertised products offered in reputable discount stores.

Beware of bait advertising. That's when a store advertises something like "Just ten armchairs at $19.98—regularly $39.98." When you get there two minutes after opening, you'll find that all ten chairs are "sold." You're offered another chair at $29.98. The $19.98 bargain never existed. That was just *bait* to bring you in. The salesman gets a bonus for selling you a higher-priced chair.

If that happens to you, squawk about it. Demand to see the department buyer, then the store president. Then tell them you're going to report them to the District Attorney, Attorney General, and State Bureau of Consumer Fraud. You'll find that a chair for $19.98 suddenly turns up. I've seen it happen.

On offers such as "double your money back," get that full double cash refund if at all dissatisfied legitimately. Make the advertiser pay. Advertisers depend on your laziness in not demanding the double refund or other big cash return. The reputable advertiser is ready to satisfy honest demands or complaints. The shady advertiser will stop making alluring guarantees if you make him pay.

Check weights and sizes of packages in your everyday shopping. For example, the Grand Union supermarket offered Carolina Extra Long Grain Rice, sixteen ounces at 19¢—and Minute Rice Pre-Cooked, fourteen ounces at 48¢. Thus, Carolina cost 1.2¢ per ounce of rice, and Minute 3.4¢ per ounce—about three times as much per ounce. That kind of thing is worth checking, especially since a fourteen-ounce "pre-cooked rice" box looks about twice as big as a sixteen-ounce box of regular rice.

With admen fighting "truth in packaging" regulations, observer Francis Loretz wrote that when a government official "made cracks about the way cereal packers were using oversize boxes to imply they contained so much contents, the packers suddenly came out with shorter boxes 'that would fit more conveniently on your pantry shelves.' Strange—the now filled-to-the-brim new packages don't shake down in transit. Could it be because freight handlers are now more careful? Ha!"

To add power to complaint letters, send copies or special letters to your favorite newspaper, columnist, magazine, commentator, wherever your story might get public attention. Speak up at club and community meetings. It works better and faster when others join with you.

As printed boldly in *Good Housekeeping:* "COMPLAIN! If a product which has earned the Good Housekeeping Consumers' Guaranty Seal is defective, tell us! We guarantee replacement or refund." In spite of this, a representative of the magazine told me that the great majority of readers with complaints don't speak up.

Advertisers of shoddy products count on your lassitude to protect them. Why let them get away with it? Standing up for what's coming to you justly is one of your "inalienable rights" in our American society. One man said, "I figure it's unpatriotic to allow myself and my family to be gypped. It means that if I don't do something about it a lot of families will be robbed the same way."

A bulletin sent out by Food Fair Stores' Jacksonville, Florida, division included a piece titled, "The Nice Customer." The essence is this: "I'm a nice customer. I never complain, no matter what kind of service I get. I'll tell you what else I am. I'm the customer who never comes back. . . ." Such "nice customers" are only partially effective. Their protests are hidden and not realized for some time by the front office where it counts most. Nothing will be improved if you don't speak up—courteously, firmly, factually.

Congresswoman Catherine May of Washington pointed the finger in stating:

> Are our legislators and federal and state agencies being flooded with complaints from all over the country? I have made a spot check on a number of occasions with colleagues who are close to consumer legislation, and I have also checked statements and

asked questions of the various bureaus in government dealing with this problem.

At no time did I get an answer that indicated that letters of complaint on any one or several consumer matters totaled more than 200 or 300. That is, on any one subject. Since we have about 182 million consumers today in the United States, I don't think we can define this as a flood. Recent publicity, including TV appearances, has urged women to write to Mrs. Peterson [then head of government consumer affairs]. But even under forced draft, the *total* is only 150 per day."

Join with others to get satisfaction. Women in Colorado joined the Housewives for Lower Prices movement, claiming to be 100,000 to 200,000 strong. They protested against high food prices and threatened to boycott food markets. Quickly the manager of a chain of forty-six stores announced, "We will close all of our stores Monday and our people will work the entire day reducing prices."

You have the strength of "about 182 million." Don't undervalue it. Don't overrate the power of a comparatively few hundreds of thousands of admen and businessmen. Each of them has only one vote, the same as you. Give your respect when warranted. Also, *demand* respect. You'll get it.

Chapter 30

ADVERTISING'S FUTURE AS IT AFFECTS YOU

The primary purpose of this book is embodied in the words of George Washington: "Truth will ultimately prevail where there is pain taken to bring it to light."

Not too many years ago, advertisers in the U.S. made claims such as the ones printed in a handbill produced recently by a firm in New Delhi for its Pifco's Saldrich Alma Hair Oil:

> It is a heavenly blessing which no words can find. It is made from Washed White Til, Olive and Almond Oils by Sun & Moon rays. Its constant use—(1) Stops hair falling off. (2) Guards against premature grayness. (3) Wards off dandruff. (4) Helps to darken the hair. (5) Keeps away all kinds of headache. (6) Keeps the brain cool and fresh, besides giving lustre to the eyes. (7) Helps proper growth of thick and long hair and adds brilliance and lustre. (8) Charms every one with its natural smell. (9) Stops casual bleeding from the nose.

No one can get away with such obvious misrepresentation for long in U.S. advertising today. Does this mean that most deception has been or will soon be eliminated? The answer is in news reports such as: "FDA Nabs Ludens Cough Drops on 'Misbrand' Charge. . . . The case was based on language on the package which says, 'Mentholated to give relief from . . . nasal congestion and catarrh, hay fever.' FDA contended the statement constitutes 'misbranding,' since the product 'is not adequate' for these purposes."

Rise Shave Cream on TV "proved" its "superior nondrying" properties when compared with "ordinary" shave cream, as two mounds of lather were shown side by side. The mound of Rise lather held its shape while the "ordinary" shave cream collapsed quickly. Checking up revealed that the "ordinary" shave cream was not shave cream. It was a special fast-drying composition of water and foaming agent put together to fall apart almost instantly.

The ambivalent attitude of advertisers is weird. The American Medical Association has long objected justifiably to exaggerated and misleading advertising of drugs, cosmetics, and health products. Yet when the AMA became an advertiser promoting their "eldercare" bill, they apparently felt that this offered license to deceive.

They were accused of exaggerating and "putting out misleading information" by one of the measure's supporters, Congressman A. S. Herlong, Jr. He said the advertisements asserted that eldercare would provide "complete coverage for those who need aid" and "100 percent of all expenses." He stated, "You know and I know that it doesn't do all those things. It is misleading."

The story is related about an adman who was telling a scientist about his work: "We act to serve the public. We seek out the finest products and present the benefits interestingly and informatively. We aim constantly to make living better for everybody."

The scientist asked, "Then you admen haven't a single fault?"

The admen blushed slightly and replied, "Well, we have one fault—we lie a little."

About this, an educator commented, "The trouble with people who think it's all right to tell little white lies is that they soon become color blind." The inevitable conclusion of any observer today must be that Madison Avenue is more than a little color blind. The concept of "legitimate puffery" is basically an evasion. It must be recognized for what it is: *Illegitimate* puffery, artifice, falsification, the permissible lie.

LeRoy Collins warned when he was president of the National Association of Broadcasters: "Unless we participate [in serving the public better], things will not come out right in the end. They will come out badly for us."

The New York *Daily News* and its advertising agency boasted of a "first" in the field. They signed up a notorious murder trial defendant, Candy Mossler, who was later acquitted, to appear in radio and TV spots and subway posters which promoted the *News* trial coverage. The attitude of the admen involved was that anything goes which will sell more product, newspapers in this instance. Another adman commented: "It proves again that no matter how bad some ads have been in the past, you'll see worse."

As a further low in bad taste, a girdle manufacturer advertised a "Stars 'n' Stripes" girdle with eight blue stars on a white background and red and white vertical stripes. A critic condemned the girdle, calling it "a shocking caricature" of the United States flag. Another complained that this was hitting women "below the belt." A more liberal commentator said about the patriotic girdle: "Long may it wave!"

Many leading admen act as if they are unaware of the distortions, bad taste, and fakery that are still perpetrated. Dan Seymour, president of J. Walter Thompson, told the Economic Club of Detroit: "We [in advertising] are among the few people who can go home every night knowing that we have done something to make the world better."

The advertising fraternity must learn that freedom of action for themselves necessarily embodies full responsibility toward the public, not token measures or actions. Chief Justice Holmes, as quoted often by President Johnson, explained: "Freedom of speech does not give a person the right to shout 'fire' in a crowded theater." Freedom of action does not give advertising the right to lie, to misrepresent, to try to push the public around in behalf of its own responsibility to business profits.

Effective progress toward truthfulness is blocked principally by each adman refusing to assume his share of responsibility for advertising evils. Instead, each points at someone else as being at fault. This was demonstrated again at a meeting of the Association of National Advertisers.

Fairfax M. Cone, chairman of the executive committee of Foote, Cone and Belding, said that "there is one place, and only one place to put the final responsibility for honest, tasteful advertising. This is with the *media*."

At the same meeting, Lee M. Rich, then senior vice president in charge of radio-TV programming and media at Benton and Bowles, blamed bad TV programming on *advertisers* who "willingly abdicated all responsibility" to the networks.

Henry Schachte, then executive vice president of J. Walter Thompson, spread the blame for ad evils, including projection of unfounded claims, on *advertisers, agencies, and media.*

This is the habitual confusing ploy of blaming everybody and everything but doing little of productive value about anything. It is so much easier to point a finger than to lift a finger. Here's what usually happens when specific action is called for. Mr. Cone urged that all advertisers should "insist, as a prerequisite for your business, that all media monitor advertising to the end that each new competitive claim written into any advertising campaign shall be accompanied by adequate, acceptable proof filed with the medium as a matter of course."

Sound reasonable? An agencyman's reaction to this: "Ridiculous! We would then be giving the power to magazines, newspapers, TV and any other media to censor our advertising mercilessly. Who the hell are they to tell us what is truth or good taste? Their meat may be our poison."

A top magazine publisher told me: "Everybody seems to bypass the obvious point that no censorship would even have to be discussed if all ads were created to tell the truth instead of trying to deceive."

I asked, "What else is new?"

He shrugged. "Realistically it's impossible for any magazine or other media to check every advertiser's claims in detail. We'd have to spend millions maintaining laboratories, scientists, experts in every advertiser's business, in hundreds of different fields. Otherwise how could we analyze their claims precisely?"

He paused, frowned. "Furthermore, we'd be wrangling endlessly with advertisers and with agencies. They're our clients, our customers, our bread and butter. They're not people we can kick around, for God's sake! We censor them? That's sheer fantasy."

"Ring-a-Round-a-Rosy"—the Madison Avenue theme song. Point the finger at the one who points back at you. If past history is permitted to repeat itself, the merry-go-round will neither stop nor break down. It will keep going round and round in a dizzying whirl of fakery and evasion as heretofore. A few voices in the field will cry despairingly for improvement, trying to be heard above the raucous din of advertising in action. Right now the calls are about as effective as howling in an empty tunnel—lots of noise, nobody hearing.

S. J. Paul, publisher of *Television Age,* explained: "What the responsible leaders in advertising are battling for is a standard of ethics that will change a defensive attitude to a positive posture." No desirable change will come about as long as the Madison Avenue definition remains that ethics are something the other fellow should live up to.

The Advertising Association of the West (AAW) adopted a ten-point "code of truth." Point three stated: "Avoid deception through implication or omission. Reveal material facts, the deceptive concealment of which might cause the consumer to be misled."

Is there any slightest chance that most admen—West, East, North, or South—will adhere to such a sterling rule? Did the advertisers and agencies which drew up and agreed to their twenty-point "rules of conduct" and ten-point "code of truth" expect anyone to follow the rules and code? Not according to past and current performance. It looks good in print—"excellent public relations."

Dr. George Gallup, honored researcher and former agencyman, has warned advertisers against continuing to think of the mass of consumers as "stupid and gullible." He said: "This view of the people is responsible for some of the greatest errors now being made in advertising, politics, and by the mass media . . . far more mistakes are being made and will be made in downgrading the mass of people than will be made in assuming that they have reached a level of taste and culture and understanding unwarranted by the facts."

Pointing out that enormous advances have been made in education and other phases of living and knowledge, Dr. Gallup urged advertising and business: "It is, therefore, vital that we take a new look at the world about us and re-examine every concept and practice bearing upon the public's interests, tastes and behavior."

It is clear that you, the individual, must decide what action you will take in respect to combatting the evils of advertising, TV programming and commercials, and other subjects covered here. You are not and never will be the puppet of advertising, business, or any other special interests or persons—as long as you don't permit yourself to be.

Thomas Jefferson said: "The mass of mankind has not been born with saddles on their back, nor a favored few booted and spurred, ready to ride them legitimately, by the grace of God." Nor by the grace of Madison Avenue.

Contradictions must be fought constantly. Governor Rockefeller pledged to protect and improve the scenic values of New York State. Simultaneously, to promote the new lottery, the state budgeted $1.5 million for advertising and public relations including "perhaps the largest billboard campaign in the state's history." What matter that roadside billboards block out nature's beauty?

It is up to you to recognize, nourish, and protect *all* your precious individual rights. Don't let any downgrader ever get away with telling you that you're but an organized, regimented unit in a giant business-ruled, advertising-dominated, computerized system. It has never been so. It is not so today. It won't be in the future—if you fight for your rights, as noted here.

Chapter

PREDICTIONS ABOUT THINGS-TO-COME IN ADVERTISING

31

"Remember this," a statesman advised, "and be well persuaded of its truth: the future is not in the hands of Faith, but in ours."

In the future, hopefully you will become more effectively resentful of smart-aleck, talk-down, demeaning, and fraudulent advertising. You will make it more specifically your business to buy products that please you both in quality and advertising approach. You will protest more. You will boycott even satisfactory products if the advertising irritates, insults, or defrauds you.

Self-regulation by advertisers and agencies will make some advances, but not enough to clear up questionable and fraudulent aspects of campaigns and ads.

The government will necessarily have to play a more intrusive role in preventing fraud in advertising. Government bodies will need and be given increased power to enforce their rulings with severe, meaningful punishment—unless Madison Avenue proves speedily by effective action that it can keep its own street clean.

The prospect for real improvement in TV programming is dismal, as things stand. *TV Guide* suggested that networks undertake a competition "to present a well-balanced schedule as well as to attract the highest ratings, competition to offer viewers programs that will exercise their minds as well as their eyes, competition to fulfill the potentialities of television that we glimpse only from time to time." The editorial concluded: "Unfortunately, it's a dream."

As matters stand, TV programming will continue to be controlled primarily by and for advertisers and agencies, as stations and networks are operated for profits above all other considerations. Public-service programming will lag far behind, kept at whatever little is considered sufficient by owners to retain their licenses.

Unless the current network view changes to an attitude that programming should be "leveled up" instead of "leveled down," the prime evening hours will continue to be filled mainly by programs that tend to downgrade rather than uplift.

It seems inevitable, based on sales results, that gradually an increasing number of advertisers will back the few shows of higher quality. They are learning slowly that better programs attract viewers who have the interest and capacity to buy more of the sponsored products than audiences three or more times in size.

More viewers will complain like Macbeth: "Out damned spot! Out I say!" If enough of you protest, as suggested, there will be a diminishing of ills—less crowding of too many commercials, less pitching of commercials louder than the program content, and less production of irritating, offensive, repetitive commercials.

Essential legal restrictions on TV commercial time are stymied in Congress. Advertisers and broadcasters are doing everything possible that money can buy to prevent such "government interference." You can demand changes and get them if you act. Shaw's words fling the brutally blunt challenge: "Get what you like—or you'll be forced to like what you get."

With all their flaws and inanities, how do advertising campaigns help increase sales, which they do unquestionably? The reason lies not in creative ability primarily but in the weight of m-o-n-e-y, over $15 billion expended on advertising annually. Even the weakest, phoniest ad mentions the product name which finally filters into the numbed ear and the glazed eye. According to a statistic provided by a Harvard Business School report, *85 percent of ads don't get looked at, are simply ignored.*

"We've got troubles," Paul C. Harper, Jr., president of Needham, Harper and Steers (Number 21), told a session of the American Association of Advertising Agencies regarding results of "a study of public attitudes toward advertising." The troubles he referred to were due to the fact that people are not reacting to advertising as admen wish—"Most of the time they don't do anything."

The agency head warned: "It means we'd better get down to business and do more of what we get paid to do: more communicating." William J. Colihan of Young and Rubicam asserted: "What admen should do is to stop trying to relate society to their business and start relating their business to society." It remains to be seen whether the gray-flannel mind is capable of really communicating with people instead of just "advertising" at them.

Regarding political advertising, a matter for deep concern is this vital fact: A campaign for a bad product fails eventually because when the product fails the purchaser, he doesn't buy again. Not so with politics. If advertising helps sell a bad candidate, the people are stuck with him for years. They can't discard him quickly like an unsatisfactory detergent.

The myth of Madison Avenue "supermen/manipulators" should now finally be exploded by the facts presented. This is of towering importance because, in the words of John F. Kennedy, "The great enemy of truth is . . . the myth."

Many admen, who object to the particular examples of their work criticized here, will state: "We're not running that campaign any more." The words in the ads may change, but as long as asininity, deception, and fraud continue, the indictments are relevant.

I'm hopeful that this *inside* truth about advertising, illuminating both the evils and benefits, may mark the beginning of an end to the preponderance of phoniness and fakery in the field. Looking back over my years in advertising, my conviction grows that the deceit, the fraud, and the smart-aleck gimmickry are not only deplorable but also fruitless and unnecessary.

Many admen are smart, able, and hard working, yet most live in a miasma of self-doubt, confusion, and insecurity. Each time a Madavenuer makes his mark in the rat race, he worries because he is surrounded by ruthlessly ambitious men with erasers. It is all so needless. It stems inherently from the basic polluted air of deception that permeates the frantic approach to preparing advertising.

Every adman and businessman must ask himself whether he feels a true sizable social responsibility. If so, he must prove by positive actions, not empty words, that he does *not* go along with this too-common negative stance:

"Any business attempt at social responsibility in my opinion is phony," said Arnold H. Maremont, president of the Maremont Corporation, makers of automotive parts and textile machines. He told the New York Chapter of the Public Relations Society of America: "It is the responsibility of business to make a profit. It is the responsibility of government to see that management conducts its business within the law and, if the law does not protect the public adequately, to create new laws."

A Change to Responsible Ethics: To admen and all businessmen I urge that they consider "ethics" not just a word, but in the full meaning expressed by Albert Schweitzer: "Ethics means concern not only with our own welfare but also with that of others, and with that of human society as a whole . . . improvement of the condition of this world."

I believe that most advertising people, not as part of the Madison Avenue pack, but as individuals, have a conscience and a strong sense of national patriotism. Much gain could be made if each were to think and work and act for the benefit of the whole public rather than solely for the advertiser.

My aim in revealing advertising's immorality and irresponsibility here is not only to serve the public, but also to aid advertising and the business world. My hope is to help spur agencymen and advertisers to concentrate more on contributing to the whole national welfare as a more beneficial social force.

Advertising need *not* forsake its responsibility to business profit. Admen and businessmen *can* change their one-sided outlook and give an increasingly large proportion of their consideration and decision-making to their responsibility to the public.

To sum up, advertising's goal should be energetic, positive idealism. We must recognize and change the young people's lack of confidence in the future of their own society. Advertising and business have enormous power for good or evil in this area.

To the basic ancient question: "If I am not for myself, who will be for me?" must be added the corollary: "But if I am only for myself, what good am I?" and finally: ". . . if not now, when?" *Some day* is no longer good enough; the time for placing public good before private gain is here.

My hope is that this book, revealing the clear, simple truth to the public and to admen and businessmen, will help shift the future emphasis in advertising in three ways:

1. To aim to tell the truth instead of seeking and promoting the permissible lie.

2. To address people as respected, thinking individuals rather than as a mass of insensitive idiots.

3. To change emphasis in creating and using advertising *first* to serve the public best, and *second* to make the sale and boost profits for business.

If these basic, all-important shifts of emphasis are undertaken and followed through, the gains for *both* public and business will be a meaningful step forward for this nation and all people everywhere, including our youngsters. I am convinced that if adherence to the permissible lie vanishes, our entire moral structure will improve.

Inevitably the precept must triumph that "Business exists for man and not man for business. The person as a person is never to be used as a means."

INDEX